Superpowers, Rogue States and Terrorism

Superpowers, Rogue States and Terrorism

Countering the Security Threats to the West

Paul Moorcraft

Pen & Sword
MILITARY

First published in Great Britain in 2017 by
Pen & Sword Military
an imprint of
Pen & Sword Books Ltd
47 Church Street
Barnsley
South Yorkshire
S70 2AS

ISBN 978 1 47389 472 3

A CIP catalogue record for this book is
available from the British Library.

Printed and bound in England
By TJ International Ltd, Padstow

Pen & Sword Books Ltd incorporates the Imprints of Pen & Sword Archaeolo-
gy, Atlas, Aviation, Battleground, Discovery, Family History, History, Maritime,
Military, Naval, Politics, Railways, Select, Transport, True Crime, Fiction, Frontline
Books, Leo Cooper, Praetorian Press, Seaforth Publishing, Wharncliffe and White
Owl.

For a complete list of Pen & Sword titles please contact
PEN & SWORD BOOKS LIMITED
47 Church Street, Barnsley, South Yorkshire, S70 2AS, England
E-mail: enquiries@pen-and-sword.co.uk
Website: www.pen-and-sword.co.uk

About the author

D r Paul Moorcraft has been a professor, paramilitary policeman, film producer and political pundit as well as a Whitehall warrior and a war correspondent. He is the author of over 30 books of fiction and non-fiction. For five years he was a senior instructor at the Royal Military Academy, Sandhurst, and later the UK Joint Services Command and Staff College. He also taught full-time (consecutively) at ten major universities in the US, UK, Africa, Australia and New Zealand. He also worked in 30 war zones, sometimes for the UK Ministry of Defence but more often as a correspondent for TV, radio and print. Besides awards for fiction, his charity work resulted in a 2015 book: *It Just Doesn't Add Up: Explaining Dyscalculia and Overcoming Number Problems for Children and Adults.* He is best known as a military historian, however. His most recent books for Pen and Sword include:

Mugabe's War Machine (2011).

Total Destruction of The Tamil Tigers: The Rare Victory of Sri Lanka's War (2012).

Omar al-Bashir and Africa's Longest War (2015).

The Rhodesian War: 50 Years on from UDI (2015) – with Peter McLaughlin.

Dying for the Truth: The Concise History of Frontline War Reporting (2016).

The Jihadist Threat: The Re-conquest of Europe? (Updated, revised paperback edition, 2017).

Contents

List of maps

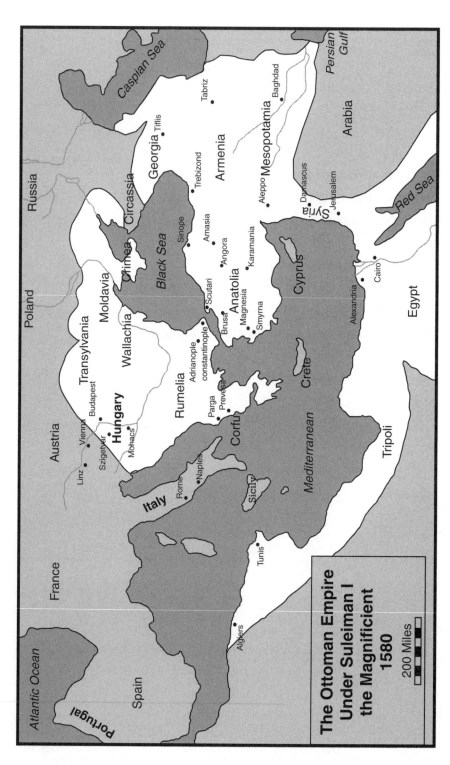

The threat to Europe from the Ottoman Empire.

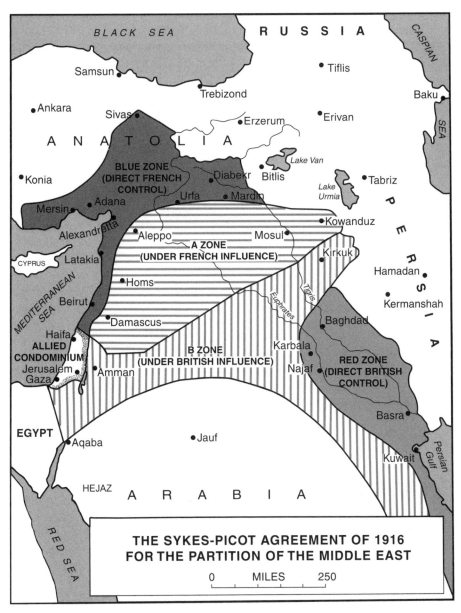

The Sykes-Picot Agreement of 1916.

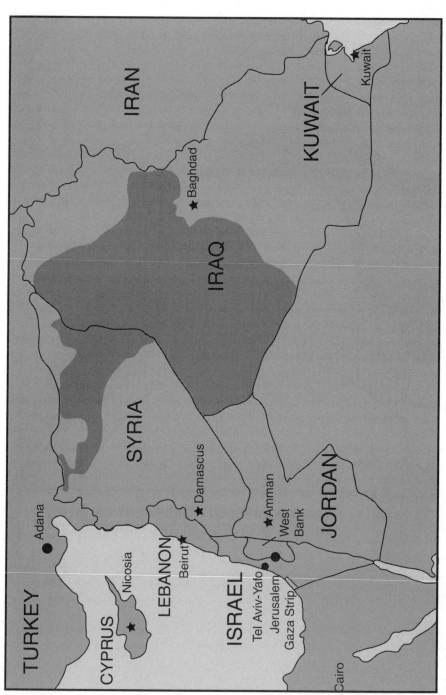

Islamic State territory in June 2014.

A possible Kurdistan.

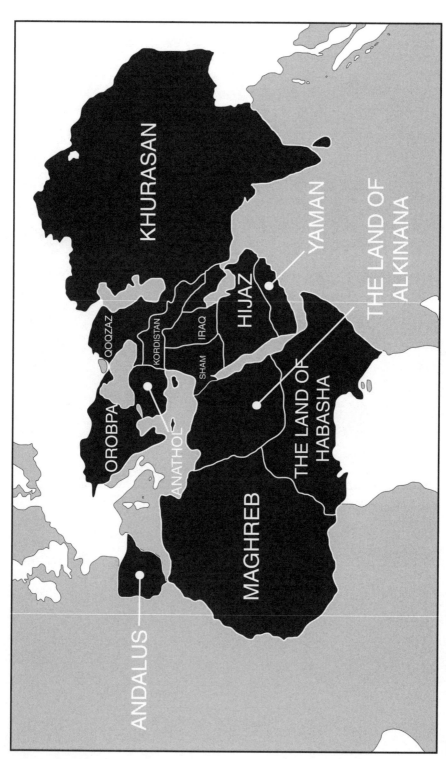

The once and future caliphate.

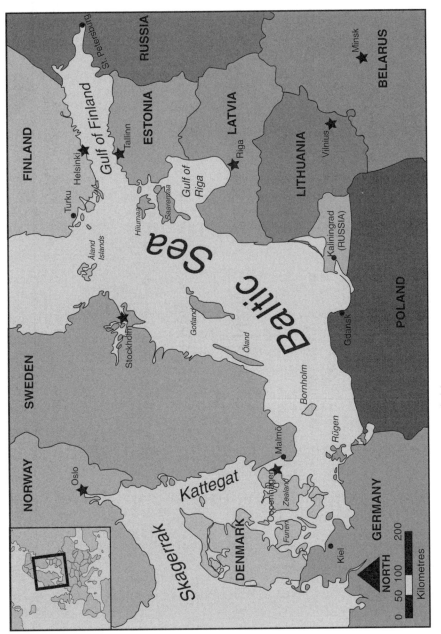

The Baltic states and their big near neighbour.

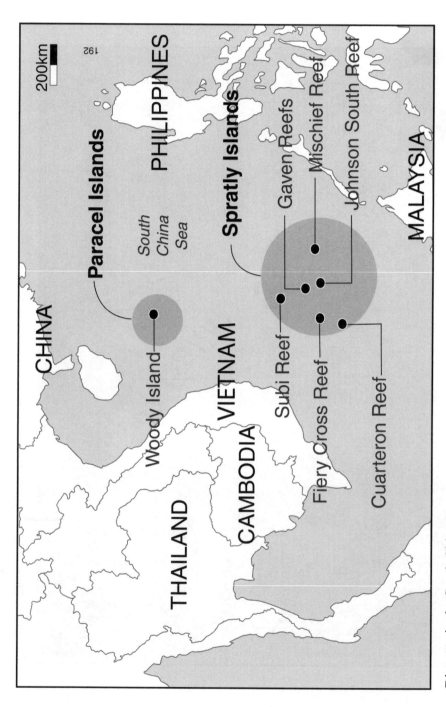

Disputes in the South China Sea.

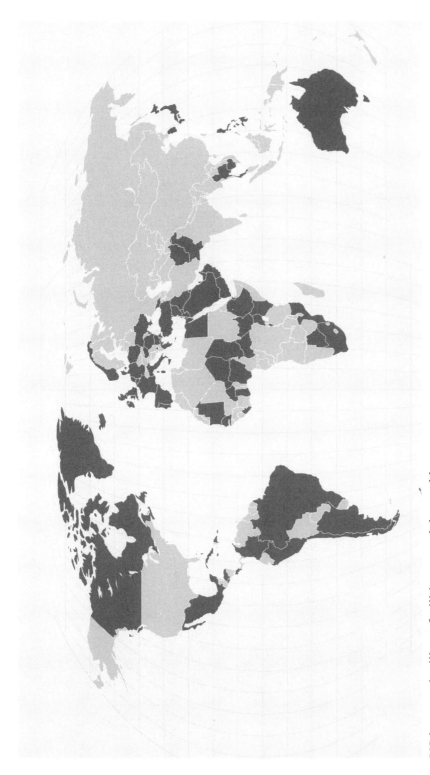

US bases and military facilities around the world.

List of illustrations

1. The Moroccan ambassador to London, sent to persuade Queen Elizabeth I to form an Anglo-Moroccan front against Spain.
2. Gertrude Bell should be more famous than Lawrence of Arabia for forging the shape of the Middle East.
3. Memorial in Washington D.C. to commemorate the US dead in the Korean War.
4. The former KGB HQ in Lukiškės Square in Vilnius, the Lithuanian capital.
5. After walking out of Afghanistan, *Mujahedin* relax in the tribal area between Afghanistan and Pakistan.
6. Ukrainian military museum, near Kiev, shows how intertwined Russian and Ukrainian defence production has been – especially in helicopter design.
7. Palestinian woman sits stoically outside her ruined house during the siege of Jenin, in the West Bank, in May 2002.
8. The fall of the Berlin Wall did not bring an 'end of history'.
9. The first Chechen war (1994–96).
10. British troops on patrol near Umm Qasr in the first weeks of the occupation of southern Iraq, 2003.
11. The Americans used cruise missiles to destroy the Al-Shifa medical factory in Khartoum in August 1998.
12. NATO forces patrolling over Afghanistan.
13. Islamic State liked to compare their initial advance with the military victories of the first caliphate.
14. German armoured vehicle in Kabul with NATO forces in 2002.
15. Islamic State forces celebrating early victories in Raqqa, their capital.

xx   Superpowers, Rogue States and Terrorism

16. The caliphate was declared on 29 June 2014 by the new caliph, Abu-Bakr al-Baghdadi.
17. GCHQ in Cheltenham, England, is the centre of British cyber warfare and defence.
18. Islamists often criticised Muslim participation in UK elections because they were considered hostile to Sharia law.
19. Front cover of *Dabiq*, the glossy propaganda magazine produced by IS.
20. Anti-Gaddafi graffito in Tripoli in the uprising during the Arab Spring.
21. The Eurofighter Typhoon was deployed in combat in Libya and is now operational in the Baltic states.
22. B-2 Spirit stealth bomber.
23. HMS *Queen Elizabeth*, the new Royal Navy carrier, but with no planes to adorn its deck, yet.
24. Kim Jong-un: 'Is that the US Navy out there?'
25. China's first aircraft carrier, the *Liaoning*.
26. Massoud Barzani, the president of Iraqi Kurdistan.
27. Michel Houellebecq, controversial French author of *Submission*.
28. President Trump has relied on a number of generals, especially H.R. McMaster, his National Security Adviser.
29. The bogus photo-shopped picture that went viral on the Internet.
30. This went viral.
31. The concept design of the Russian T-14 Armata tank.

Saving the West

The West would inevitably collapse under the weight of its own contradictions. This is what Vladimir Lenin prophesied a century ago. Yet the Soviet Union he helped to create imploded long before serious tensions in the capitalist system threatened the West's demise. Lenin had forged his revolution when Russia was swamped in one of the greatest wars mankind had ever suffered. Under Joseph Stalin, Lenin's even more ruthless successor, the Soviet Union overcame another German invasion; despite huge losses, the Red Army drove the enemy all the way back to Berlin and brought the whole of central and eastern Europe under its control.

Since then Western Europe has been largely at peace. The original European Community, fusing the raw sinews of the historical war machines, the coal and steel industries, was designed specifically to prevent military conflict between France and Germany. And that *has* worked. So far. Not a single member of the expanded European Community has gone to war with another member state. As some former inmates of the Soviet empire joined the EU and also the North Atlantic Treaty Organisation, Europe looked secure. The old enemy Russia dwindled into strategic insignificance. It appeared as if the long civil war in Europe (1914-1990) had finally ended – peacefully.

America bestrode the world as the sole superpower; it was uniquely powerful and yet also simultaneously uniquely vulnerable. Suddenly the heartland of the Western system – the US – was blindsided by an Islamist masterstroke. Some of New York's and Washington's most iconic buildings, including the Pentagon, were attacked by al-Qaeda. A small guerrilla group had declared war on the remaining superpower: this was asymmetric warfare with a vengeance. Shocked and angered by this first attack on the homeland since Pearl Harbor, the American war machine went into overdrive with the so-called 'war on terror'. The ensuing invasions of Afghanistan and Iraq convulsed the Muslim world, firing up, not extinguishing, extreme Islamic militancy.

In 2000 Vladimir Putin came to power in Moscow with the aim of restoring his country's self-respect and military prowess. Russian forces redrew borders in Georgia, then Ukraine. This was the first time European borders had been changed by force since Hitler. Then the Russian military intimidated the Baltic states, although Moscow in turn complained of NATO encirclement. In 2015 Putin intervened dramatically in Russia's long-term ally, Syria, and changed the balance of power in favour of President Bashar al-Assad, who had faced possible defeat at the hands of a kaleidoscope of Syrian rebels and foreign powers. Putin was rewriting not just borders, but rewiring the post-1945 world order and international legal system.

After 2008 the economic crisis caused by the banking collapse inspired nightmare flashbacks of the Great Crash of 1929. The capitalist system survived – just. Then the EU's common currency, the euro, started to crumble, especially in the weaker economies, notably Greece, but also Spain and Italy. For the time being, German economic might could buttress its floundering neighbours. Then the widespread chaos in the Middle East, with its epicentre in Syria, propelled millions, mainly Muslims, to seek refuge in Europe. The disintegration of the Libyan state has resulted in a borderless black hole for the people smugglers who are funnelling African refugees and migrants, not just from destitute and war-torn states such as South Sudan and Eritrea, but also relatively prosperous though misgoverned countries such as Nigeria. Parts of the EU hastily restored many of their former border demarcations in a wild orgy of fence-building. Partly because of the refugee crisis and disillusionment with the democratic deficits in the soul of the EU administration, in June 2016 Britain voted to leave the EU but not its commitments to Europe in general and to NATO in particular. Britain's departure boosted the wave of right-wing populism that engulfed Europe. Then the most politically and militarily inexperienced presidential candidate in modern history won the US presidency in November 2016. 'The Donald' promised to utterly change how NATO operated – the US was not going to carry the military shirkers in the alliance any more. Then, in December 2016, Italy voted 'no' in a constitutional referendum that seemed to echo Brexit.

The West finds itself in economic, military and political turmoil. So why shouldn't Russia capitalise on the disarray? The Baltic states and parts of Poland that had once been Russian a long time ago appeared to be on Putin's shopping list. Although the caliphate of the Islamic State was staggering under the firepower of coalition forces, it managed to strike at the heart of Europe. Spectacular Islamist terror attacks hit Belgian, German, French and then British cities.

To many of its proponents, Brexit meant that the UK was jumping from a sinking ship. Whether the departure from the EU was of negative or positive benefit to Britain, London would be blamed for catalysing the termination of the European dream. At the same time the election of the most divisive and unpopular American president in modern times, Donald Trump, suggested that the former *Pax Americana* could be over, not least for the more fragile and prodigal European countries that sheltered under America's nuclear umbrella.

And yet Donald Trump promised to be a very unpredictable leader. *The Washington Post*'s definitive biography of the man talked of 'the cartoon devils and angels whispering into his ears, the two forces that propelled Trump through all his life's crises – his thin skin and short temper warring against his oceanic confidence …'.[1] Trump insisted he made his own decisions. 'I understand how life works,' he said, 'I'm the Lone Ranger.' The fledgling president launched fifty-nine cruise missiles on 6 April 2017 on a Syrian air force base which had been the source of a chemical onslaught on civilians a few days earlier. He changed his long-term isolationist policy in a complete volte-face. Whether that was his own decision or whether the pictures of dead babies influenced his daughter Ivanka to persuade her father is a moot point. It was exactly the 100th anniversary of the USA's entry into the First World War. World politics had changed overnight in

1917 *and* in 2017. Then the US dropped its 'mother of all bombs', the largest non-nuclear device in the US armoury, on an underground Islamic State compound in caves in eastern Afghanistan. Next Trump ordered a carrier strike group to patrol off the coast of North Korea (though it was initially proceeding in the opposite direction). The world's media screamed headlines of possible nuclear war and a return to the alarms of the 1962 Cuban missile crisis. China and Russia would have to sit up and take notice that the USA was no longer firing blanks. In fact Moscow warned that the US strike had come within a whisker of a major clash with the Russian troops at the Syrian base hit by the American Tomahawks.

How would the old world react to the spectacular change of direction in Trump's new world? Would Europe revert to type, the beggar-your-neighbour squabbles of the inter-war years, or perhaps even the religious struggles of the Thirty Years War, if the more extreme jihadists got their way? Would Russia take back its satellites that were freed only a generation before? Was the fate of Europe inevitably bound up with that of America, the saviour that had stepped into the continent three times, to save it twice from the Germans and once from the Russians? Or would NATO break up into its jigsaw parts? President Barack Obama talked of pivoting towards the east to face the new economic and military superpower of China that had caught up with or even overtaken the American colossus. Empires rise and fall; it is the nature of *homo sapiens*. So was the West in terminal decline?

This book first asks what 'the West' is before considering whether it is in decline. My recent controversial work – *The Jihadist Threat: The Re-conquest of the West?* – examined the history of Islamic extremism from the time of the Prophet. It asked awkward questions; I was then encouraged by my publishers to try to answer them. Then Brexit and Trump certainly changed the world and therefore the focus of my book. This study deploys a wider canvas, though it will still consider the more immediate threats to the Western alliance system – not just jihadism but also the menace of Russian revanchism, for example.

Superpowers, Rogue States and Terrorism traces the growth of the Islamic threat and offers some domestic and international solutions by working with potential allies in Europe, Asia and the Middle East. The decline of 'the West' has been prophesied for as long as the term has been used. My conclusion is positive – many of the current problems can be solved. In short, Lenin is still wrong.

****

I wrote this book mainly during a self-imposed Christmas hermitage in the beautiful Surrey Hills. My small riverside cottage was warm, however, as I looked back over forty years of serving in, or *in situ* reporting on, many wars. I look out over the rolling snow-covered hills and tremble that I should possess the *chutzpah* to write about a world that is changing so dramatically, so quickly. It is a little like commenting live on the French revolution, or predicting the future of Europe in late 1918. I stuck my neck out (literally) in my previous book, *The Jihadist Threat*, published in October 2015. I thought that even if my former Islamist friends – whom I dubbed 'moderate beheaders' – did not do me in, I might take some flak from the UK security establishment. Instead the British Army put my book on a shortlist of six (from about 2,000) as the 'Military Book of the Year'. Pen and Sword asked me to provide a second work on possible solutions to Islamist terrorism. I am sure I have made many mistakes and, even where I got things right, the tempo of change may make me look out of time when the book is finally published. So please forgive my infelicities. I have simply done my best.

I would like thank my fellow Surrey Hills dwellers, Julian Graves, James Barker and Tony Denton, for their help. My old school-friend Fran Ainley gave me an insight into North Korea. And, as ever, I want to thank the various inmates and freelance editors of Pen and Sword publishers, especially Henry Wilson, Richard Doherty and Matt Jones, for their patience and support.

Surrey Hills
England
April 2017

Chapter 1

Decline of the West?

As a child of empire, and inevitably a keen philatelist of empire, I grew up with exotic geographic notions such as 'the Far East'. It is 'far' if your eyes roam from the 'Rhondda grey' in Wales across those broad swathes of pink on schoolroom maps. The West also had a rose-tinted perspective if you happened to be born in northern America or northern Europe. The West was transformed into the democratic domains of white Anglo-Saxon Protestants. Sociologist Max Weber's notions connecting Protestant work ethics and capitalism infused much of imperial thinking. Maybe it was all in the terrain – social democracy flourished in the cold climes of Scandinavia and Canada, while traditional ideals of Anglo-American financial transparency prospered less well in the warmer, and ipso facto more corrupt, southern climates of Catholic territories in southern Europe or Latin America. Such geographic (and religious) determinism largely grew less fashionable in the late-twentieth century, but not the racial superiority associated with a WASP-dominated West.

Asians, South Americans or Africans would interpret the West differently, as did the ideologues in Soviet Moscow. In 1978 Edward Said published his masterpiece, *Orientalism*; it forced Western academics and journalists to look again at the Islamic and Arab worlds. And yet the West is not just a pseudonym for the Occident or antonym for the Orient. What is it then? Most educated people might risk a rough guesstimate of what 'the West' means – perhaps 'Plato to NATO'. Or maybe 'Christendom' or 'liberal democracy'. Some might suggest 'capitalism'.

British private-school history courses would usually gallop through the cultural glories of Greece that later add a superficial lustre to the military prowess of Rome. The Roman emperors eventually made Christianity the official religion of all their territories while also quietly absorbing local deities for political and cultural convenience. In 395 the Roman Empire was divided into east and west, partly because of encroaching barbarian armies and also bloated bureaucracy. The western empire finally expired in 476. From its long-cold ashes, the Holy Roman Empire eventually emerged, which – as every schoolchild *used* to know – was not holy, not Roman nor really an empire. It survived a thousand years, however, and helped to put the papacy in its place; and so most of Europe avoided the blinkers of a theocracy. Meanwhile, the Renaissance helped to drive away the legacy of the so-called Dark Ages. Religious wars had savagely blighted European development for too long. In 1648 the Treaty of Westphalia formally ended the Thirty Years' War and introduced the concept of the individual sovereignty of modern nation states. The Enlightenment, well, it helped to enlighten the tiny minority of people who were not obsessed with finding the next crust of bread. The scientific and agricultural revolutions provided more bread, more cheaply, and turned first Britain then the empires of France and Germany into major industrial powers. In the nineteenth century Britain and France expanded their land-holdings throughout the world, sometimes at the expense of other older European imperialists such as Portugal and Spain who had taken over Latin America and parts of Africa centuries before. Germany, Italy and Belgium were latecomers to imperialism but nonetheless still fervent as all late converts are.

Until 1914 European states dominated the globe. Imperialism and Western domination co-existed as kith and kin. After the two world wars, however, America and the USSR, now both exalted to the title of 'superpower', overshadowed the planet and bisected Europe. This was the Cold War. The West was dubbed the 'first world', the USSR and its satellites the 'second world', and the third category comprised the developing and 'non-aligned' countries in Africa, Latin America and Asia. This was the high point of the modern concept of the West – the 'Free World' versus the Soviet 'evil empire', to use a phrase popularised by President Ronald Reagan. The West was largely white, superficially Christian and claiming to be democratic – according to the principles of the *demos* allegedly handed down from Athens. Of course, ancient Greece depended on slaves, who did not have the vote, and the Marxist-Leninists headlined this point, comparing ancient slavery with the modern version of captive states in the European empires. Like most generalisations, this charge contained some truth.

The USA practised slavery legally until the Civil War, and almost until the Obama presidency unofficial Jim Crow restrictions persisted. Despite its self-image as the shining city on the hill, the USA has always been a flawed democracy. As Kwame Anthony Appiah outlined in his brilliant 2016 Reith lectures on Western culture, you can't trace a straight line from the Athenian democracy to European and American liberal democracy. Much of European history has been blighted by barbaric governance and practices, and not just egregious examples such as the Spanish Inquisition. Spain, Portugal and Greece itself endured dictatorship *after* the European Community was forged and long after democracy flourished in developing countries such as India. Nor is it always useful to deploy the term 'the West' to differentiate the North Atlantic countries of North America and Europe, the apparently enlightened ones, from the global South or, especially, the Islamic world. It is important to remember that many of the Greek and Latin classics, including some of those written by Plato himself, survived only because they had been translated into Arabic during Europe's Dark Ages. Professor Appiah's Reith lectures also delved into the question of Western 'culture'. He asked, for example, whether the term 'could apply equally to Mozart and Justin Bieber, to Thomas Aquinas or Kim Kardashian'? It is a sad comment on Western 'culture' that Ms Kardashian's butt has caused far more discussion and analysis than anything its owner has said or done.

The bad news

The first volume of Oswald Spengler's famous *Decline of the West* was published in 1918. The Great War was ripping apart the heart of Europe and marking the beginning of the ascendancy of Soviet Russia and capitalist America. The unholy trinity of trenches, barbed wire and machine guns also eviscerated the Victorian and Edwardian beliefs in meliorism: that scientific and moral progress would inevitably improve modern life and *homo sapiens*. This was also the appeal of communism: terminating the oppressive state system would create paradise for all mankind, especially the workers. Instead, the mechanisation of war in 1914–18 – bomber aircraft, tanks and poison gas – introduced new technological nightmares. The belief that 'the bomber will always get through' was partly vindicated at Guernica and in the early stages of the London Blitz; it reached its zenith in the firestorms of Dresden in 1945. The Nazis' mass killings in the Holocaust destroyed belief in European civilisation. And it annihilated the faith of many: some rabbis even opined that Yaweh had also died in Auschwitz. The creed of inevitable human progress dissolved in the mushroom clouds above two Japanese cities in the last weeks of the Second World War.

Nevertheless, just as after 1918, in 1945 the cry was 'Never Again'. The western half of Europe rebuilt itself and constructed the European Union, partly to banish war from the continent. American money bankrolled the restoration of Europe which was protected by US weapons in NATO. It was unlikely that the Soviets really wanted to march all the way to the Channel but American tanks stood in their way should they choose the belligerent option. Instead, trying to keep up with US military spending helped to undermine the whole Soviet Union that collapsed – much to the surprise of nearly all Sovietologists in the West. Paul Kennedy's influential book *The Rise and Fall of the Great Powers* was pessimistic about US power because it was replicating the imperial overstretch of the *Pax Britannica*, or so he argued. And yet it was the USSR that fell apart because of this precise problem, just three years after Kennedy's book came out. Western optimists predicted then the 'end of history', and the inevitable triumph of liberal democracy. The Western democracies had won in both world wars and now the Cold War. Surely the triumph of liberal democracy was irreversible? It was not – it was soon met by the rise of autocracy in Russia and China, and also implacable theocratic authoritarianism in the Middle East. After a brief period of optimism, 'pop' pessimism took over, based on left-wing ideologies as well as very negative forecasts about the environment. The cultural output grew darker as well, especially in the cinema, from a future of 'Mad Max' to the grim robotic world of the 'Terminator'.

The US colossus bestrode the world, yet the American empire overspent its capital in too many wars, initially in Vietnam and then in the Middle East after 2001. By 2016 Donald Trump's victory apparently symbolised a retreat into US protectionism, semi-isolationism and the garrison state. By some economic indicators, China had already overtaken the US; Beijing had outplayed the master at the capitalist game, but without undermining the disciplined control of the Chinese Communist Party.

Spengler had been an early prophet of cultural pessimism; Arthur Herman's *Idea of Decline in Western History* updated and re-energised the old argument for writing off the West. In a sweeping analysis, from Freud to Madonna, Herman explained how the decline of Western civilisation had become embedded in the popular imagination. It was an easy shot to make a case for the degradation in music by analysing Madonna but in his survey of philosophers from Nietzsche to Sartre and then to Foucault he constructed a more sophisticated critique of the declinist argument.

The cultural pessimists were given a mighty boost in 2008. It was the year of the financial crash that did more damage to Western capitalism than all the abominations of al-Qaeda. In Britain parts of some big commercial banks were nationalised. When the going was good they could make huge profits for the bankers and the shareholders, but when things went wrong the poor bloody taxpayers were expected to shoulder the burden. This was welfare-state capitalism with a vengeance. Even Her Majesty, Queen Elizabeth, was heard to ask publicly why nobody had seen the financial crash coming. The left-wing had long despised the bankers; now the general public loathed them as well. Bankers were relegated in social status to below estate agents and used-car salesmen. Jokes abounded: why don't sharks attack bankers? Professional courtesy. So it was no surprise that later a suspicion of experts – especially those organisations and 'economists' who had made such a massive cock-up – should lead to Brexit and the rise of the Donald in 2016.

The year of living dangerously

Some years are clearly more significant than others: 1848 was the year of revolutions in Europe. The year 1917 marked the Russian revolution(s) and the entry of the USA into the Great War. The period 1945-46 witnessed the end of the war against Nazi Germany and the onset of the Cold War with the Soviet Union and its allies. If Putin starts the advertised war with the West in 2017, then that year, or thereabouts, may well outshine – literally – any survivor's calendar of important dates.[1]

George W. Bush and Tony Blair had inspired a decade and more of disasters in the Middle East and so Barack Obama and David Cameron tried to avoid 'boots on the ground'. Nevertheless, the intervention in Libya demonstrated that Cameron was just as eager as Tony Blair to cosy up to Washington in matters of war and peace. And yet the British House of Commons failed to support Cameron's first attempt at intervention in Syria after President Assad's alleged use of chemical weapons. This vote was an excuse for President Obama to back off from his much-trumpeted 'red line' over the use of Syrian WMD. This time, non-intervention, however, may have made the civil war in Syria worse. It was a case of damned if you do and damned if you don't. At the same time Washington did lead a coalition air war against the Islamic State. Bush's war on terror and then the Arab Spring engulfed the Islamic world from the Sahara to Pakistan. Governments fell or tottered into even greater secular authoritarianism or jihadism. An anti-Western Islamic blowback roared, and yet paradoxically many millions of Muslims risked their lives to join the massive wave of migrants who swamped Europe. Thousands of Muslims were prepared to proclaim and even die for the new caliphate, yet millions of their co-religionists risked their lives to live in the land of the infidels. Not since the end of the Second World War had the continent been so engulfed by so many columns of desperate refugees, although many in 2015-16 owned smart phones and wore designer gear. Europe could not cope with this influx, exacerbated by Chancellor Angela Merkel's noble but disastrous invitation to them. Financial crashes contributed to the fatal weakening of the euro, while the tsunami of people from the Middle East, Asia and Africa shook the foundations of the European Union.

Poorer whites in Europe and in the USA looked to their governments to solve these crises. Many in the working class white majority resented being treated as a minority in their own country. They shape-shifted from lumpenproletariat or lower middle class into a new revolutionary class. Leadership had failed and so followership changed too. Although connected, Brexit and Trumpism were different. In Britain the drive to leave the EU was led by people who were more optimistic and globally minded and not necessarily Little Englanders. Brexit offered many different, sometimes contradictory, solutions. The election of Trump for president was more negative than positive, *anybody* but 'crooked' Hillary Clinton. The fact that she won more popular votes – if not electoral college votes – showed perhaps that many Americans wished a plague on both houses.

It could be argued that America's rebellion and 240-year-old experiment in self-government had failed. Britons joked that a return to the British Crown might work better than a system where a whole country put up two final presidential contenders who were massively unpopular. Maybe the bumper stickers should say: 'Make America Great Britain Again'. Theresa May, who succeeded Prime Minister Cameron, enjoyed popularity levels that Trump or Clinton couldn't even dream of. Arguably, the Brexit victory in Britain showed that British democracy worked. The fact that Trump could win partly because of his billionaire status and TV fame in 'The Apprentice' and also because of the sheer force of his strange personality trumpeted that the US system was broken. Some commentators suggested that in both countries the plebs used their vote to tell the liberal elite to get stuffed. There is some truth in this. Daniel McCarthy, the editor of the *American Conservative,* put it thus: 'With Clinton, there is neither hope nor change. Trump may be awful, but he was awful different.'

Both popular revolutions in the US and UK would change the Western alliance. The immigration and euro crises were likely to implode the EU, so Britain was wise to leave, although Brexit would be blamed for hastening the pre-existing existential threats to the Brussels bureaucracy.

The challenged elites in Washington and London stamped their collective feet in utter horror at the Trump and Brexit victories. But the democratic decision had been made, so backsliding on departure from the EU or attempts to impeach Trump were almost bound to be self-defeating. The most important factor in both countries was to heal the massive chasm in the electorate. The *Spectator* columnist Rod Liddle condemned those who attacked pro-Brexit voters as typical of a 'hate-filled xenophobic shitbag about to go out and lamp a Pole'. (For my American readers, 'lamp' means to strike someone with force, usually in the face.)

Before the referendum on leaving or staying in the EU in June 2016, the vast majority of 'experts' in government, the World Bank and a multiplicity of economic organisations all prophesied Armageddon if Britain left the security blanket of the EU. The majority of Britons had long given up on expert opinion, especially about economics, the dismal science. It was certainly dismal but it was no science. The British economy and the stock market *improved* after Brexit, although a final verdict can be reached only when Britain has completed the inevitably long and probably bitter divorce from the EU. Suspicion of expert opinion had been nourished by a number of factors: the decline of class deference in the UK, the anger at the failed intelligence estimates that led to war in Iraq, the dislike of politicians as a result of various parliamentary expenses' scandals and, above all, the failure of almost the entire economic and political establishment to see the 2007/8 crash coming. The bankers had caused the crash but it was the poorest in society who ended up paying for the new age of austerity. Then came the warning about Brexit. This was the equivalent of the 'dodgy dossiers' about Saddam's alleged WMD. The experts – wittingly or unconsciously – were saying what their political paymasters wanted them to say. This was sexed-up 'science' with a vengeance. And when the economy improved, although the value of the pound dropped (inadvertently helping exporters), the so-called experts appeared to be mendacious self-serving toffs. This only entrenched the divisions that had partly caused Brexit.

Not only were economic values questioned. The whole international system was in turmoil. For the first time since 1945 many states, great and small, were in thrall to various sorts of chauvinism and nationalism. The world has been experiencing globalisation *and* increasing regionalisation. With Trump in Washington, relations with Russia looked set to improve. Yet Russia, as well as Turkey and China, had recently embraced a zero-sum view of global politics. Within the EU the old borders were literally being resurrected not least to stop the flood of refugees as well as to block Islamist terrorism. The poorer southern states could quit the euro and even the EU. Italy and even France showed signs of wanting to opt out of the club. And the hub of European power, Germany, was questioning its traditional passive international role, and even permanent penitence about Nazism.

America had always regarded the EU as a natural component of the Washington-led defence architecture. British Brexiteers had insisted that they were committed to NATO. The new commander in chief, Donald J. Trump, had openly questioned the NATO alliance, however, defining it as a military welfare state. The allies did little and paid even less, while Uncle Sam shouldered the burden, again. Trump was largely correct in this stark analysis. It was time for the Western allies of the US to do much more, especially as the Cold War Mark 2 became far more dangerous, with the increase of NATO forces in Eastern Europe and the Baltic states. *Pax Americana* could even be on the way out. The Brits, with a new political independence and a so-called 'independent' nuclear deterrent, may be required to take a bigger military role in defending a fragmenting Europe. The EU might need Britain more than vice versa, especially the dominant financial role of the City of London. So the economic and military arguments might make the actual British exit a little 'softer'.

The decline in cultural or economic influence the West can exert is not as important as hard power. The West, including the USA, has arguably suffered a decline in military power as well.

Chapter 2

Law of the Jungle

One of the most influential books written recently about political decline is Paul Kennedy's *The Rise and Fall of the Great Powers*, first published in 1987 and briefly discussed in the previous chapter. Kennedy was a specialist in naval history and used expenditure on navies as one of the key measures of imperial waxing and waning. The metric still applies – especially to the country which once possessed the world's largest navy – Britain. At the time of writing, Britain doesn't have a single operational aircraft carrier. It will do soon but it won't have any aircraft to fly off the damn thing. The promised two carriers are the biggest warships ever commissioned for the Royal Navy, the size of ten football pitches. They have certainly provided jobs for Scottish shipyards. After the carrier deals were signed in 2008 it was mooted initially that only one ship would be built and then the original two would go ahead, perhaps one for the Royal Navy and one jointly deployed with the French navy. The British possibly needed only one but political pressures kept both in play partly because the Scottish nationalists were running rampant, first in the local Scottish parliamentary elections, and then in 2015 the SNP almost swept the board in the national Westminster elections (winning 56 out of 59 parliamentary seats).

The carriers, however, are 'less relevant to Britain's security needs than is the Great Pyramid', to quote Sir Max Hastings. Famously, the Royal Navy has had more admirals than ships. In 2017 the media are complaining of British warships that Russian subs can hear 100 miles away, drones costing £1 billion that have not entered service twelve years after being ordered and new light tanks that are too big to fit into some planned transport aircraft. And, meanwhile, British generals have not stood up to politicians' military fantasies, not least that big cuts in regulars can be compensated for by notional reserves. In 2015 more Brits were trying to join the Islamic State forces than the British Army's reserves, once called the TA (Territorial Army). Far worse is the large number of unnecessary and usually spurious legal enquiries about British conduct in Iraq. It is truly disgusting how poorly paid young people (far below the living wage) have been sent by politicians to fight in two calamitous wars and then the government allows, even encourages, the prosecution of these sometimes traumatised service men and women, perhaps to salve politicians' consciences.

In 2016 the UK Ministry of Defence had more pieces of fine art than it had tanks, warships, submarines and aircraft. The MoD boasted 2,145 pictures, sculptures and antique furniture. It also owned six eighteenth-century marine clocks with a combined value of £52 million. It also held very valuable paintings by William Hodges, the artist who accompanied Captain James Cook during the exploration of the Pacific in the 1770s. It might be an idea to sell some real antiques to fund the replacement of other antiques that are still flying in the RAF. It may have been an implicit government decision, certainly with the Tory-Lib Dem coalition in 2010, to enfeeble the armed forces so much that they would not be able to fight big wars again. Maybe that was OK for the Middle East but not when it came to defend the homeland.

Of course hard power isn't just about up-to-date military hardware and even the size of the armed forces; it's also about the guts to use the ships, tanks and fighter aircraft. Europe obviously and the USA less obviously have been suffering deficits in both: intention and capability. The end of the (first) Cold War encouraged many European countries to run down their armed forces. Even relatively big military powers such as the UK argued that they wouldn't do major wars again – except alongside America-led NATO. So military capacity across the whole spectrum made less sense – let European nations specialise, it was decided. That was potentially smart, except that budgets were not maintained in this culture of a race to the bottom. The standardisation of equipment was poor, for example, despite decades of so-called reform. The twenty-eight EU members boasted twelve types of tanker aircraft and nineteen kinds of fighters. NATO militaries have been cursed with duplication and redundancy. Few sustained the agreed 2 per cent of GDP spending on defence. Even Britain, which claimed it did, massaged the figures by including, for example, intelligence spending that was previously excluded. And what they did spend was sometimes wasted.

Britain currently spends a mandated 0.7 per cent of its GNP on overseas aid via the Department for International Development (DfID). Much of this money has been ill-used previously on large sums given to projects in China and India which were not needed or even wanted in India's case. Critics of DfID asked: why should Britain be giving aid to countries with big space programmes and nuclear arsenals? The critics also said that India had an aircraft carrier when Britain didn't. Fortunes have been poured down the drain in Africa, most famously recently supporting a female singing group in Ethiopia. Western aid in general has created an army of NGO-istas in Africa, far more people than the number of imperial civil servants at the height of European colonialism.

DfID should return to the FCO after giving up at least half of its aid budget to the Ministry of Defence. Some of the new money could be spent on peacebuilding, for example on military operations to help refugees in South Sudan. Judicious use of this extra money would not only satisfy taxpayers but also the 'stretched' 2 per cent defence budget could be pushed to a genuine 3 per cent. That would please everyone, not least the Americans (though it would upset the diehard spendaholics in the DfID bureaucracy). Perhaps 5 per cent of this huge aid budget could also be given to supplement food banks in the UK. Charity should always begin at home.

*****

General Jim Mattis, Trump's defence secretary, famously warned NATO that 'Americans cannot care more for your children's security than you do … . If your nations do not want to see America moderate its commitment to this alliance, each of your capitals need to show support for common defence'. Defence spending in NATO can be like comparing apples and pears. It may be possible to spend the same or even less money but stop wasteful duplication. The French will stubbornly buy French tanks not German ones even if they are better. Also missions should be redefined. NATO's European members, except Britain, largely kept out of the 2003 invasion of Iraq but expended much blood and treasure in Afghanistan. They did a fair amount of heavy lifting in the Libyan war. The Americans tend not to fully appreciate the extent to which NATO and EU states have engaged in numerous peacekeeping, policing and monitoring roles – in the Balkans especially, but also Georgia, Sudan, the Sahel, the Gaza strip, and the waters of the Med and in the Indian Ocean. If the French especially had not committed numerous military assets to North Africa (for example Mali) the US would have struggled to pick up the pieces, let alone the local knowledge. Europe also has to provide large amounts of sometimes free facilities for American forces as well as massive – and justifiable – contributions to the NATO Infrastructure Programme. It is much easier for American forces to deploy from the European 'lily pads' to the Middle East or Southwest Asia than to travel from the USA. Having said that, it is clear that the Europeans need to do far more to defend themselves. And although Britain likes to parade its – sort of – commitment to the 2 per cent NATO spending goals, it still falls short in other areas.

In 2016 Britain had *no* designated maritime reconnaissance aircraft; along with a shortage of hunter-killer submarines; that is why General Shirreff's controversial factional book about the imminent war with Russia highlighted Putin's sinking of the British carrier, HMS *Queen Elizabeth*. Even economic basket cases such as Greece managed to keep to the 2 per cent but squandered their money on excessive military pensions, not modern technology. Besides Greece and the UK (arguably) only tiny Estonia and the giant US stepped up to the 2 per cent mark, although Poland had just got its act together. All NATO powers had cut their budgets massively after the fall of the Berlin Wall. Despite some minor recent improvements because of Russian bellicosity, it is still only the US that does the heavy lifting by paying 73 per cent of NATO's overall budget. In the 'coalition' war against Islamic State, the US conducts 90 per cent of the air strikes.

The Pentagon has nagged its NATO allies repeatedly but it too has not fully modernised its own weapons systems since Ronald Reagan's buying spree thirty years ago. Classic examples are the M1 Abram tanks and F-16 fighters. The specialised American bomber force has fallen by half. Until the very recent mobilisation to support the Baltics, the USA did not have a single immediately operational tank in Europe. During the Cold War the US Army could field 5,000 tanks ready for use. The attacks on the Twin Towers and the consequent heavyweight expeditionary wars in Afghanistan and Iraq improved tactics, especially by deploying drones, and yet the campaigns also degraded much of the conventional equipment. Some of the NATO members' efforts were merely tokens: the Danish army's contribution to NATO operations in Helmand consisted of four Leopard tanks – one hit an IED and the so-called Danish 'armoured corps' was 25 per cent down for a long time; though those who served in Helmand always spoke very highly of the Danes. It is commonplace to say that the Blair/Bush wars and Cameron's Libyan escapade have exhausted European patience with expeditionary warfare, especially military intervention in Muslim countries. And yet this war weariness or wariness, although understandable, means that NATO cannot defend its eastern borders properly, and that Britain's mainland is under-protected: against major-power threats, say, from the Russians *and* terrorist infiltration. So many so-called 'out-of-area' operations have meant that the NATO core area is dangerously vulnerable.

I worked inside both the MoD in Whitehall and in the defence procurement HQ in Abbey Wood on the outskirts of Bristol. Over 6,000 inmates then worked in Abbey Wood and I came to believe that the best thing to do to improve efficiency was to sack 3,000 and dramatically increase the salaries of the other half. Admittedly, that was in 2000. Despite unceasing bureaucratic reforms I am not convinced that much has improved. It is true that defence procurement has been a problem for nearly all advanced nations. Projects are nearly always way over budget and often 'gold-plated' – service chiefs want the kit to do nearly everything. Inter-service rivalry tends to exacerbate turf wars caused by arguments over gold-plated pet projects. And when it came to the costs of the carriers there was a pattern of navy personnel over-specifying the kit and underestimating the costs and expecting that somebody else would pay. That was the MoD way. Of even more concern is the navy will not have enough destroyers, frigates and subs to protect the new carriers. A few cynics argue that the carriers, which cost upwards of £6.2 billion each (up from £3.7 billion in 2007), will be vulnerable to new missile systems such as the Chinese DF-21 which has a range of 1,100 miles.

Britain has had some procurement disasters in the past and the standard reply is for the MoD and government ministers to resort to variations on the argument of 'force multiplier'. 'We may have far fewer of this or that new piece of kit but it is five/ten times more powerful than its predecessors so we can make up for lack of numbers by the extra firepower.' This was dubbed 'more bang for the buck'.

The Americans have done the same but naturally on a grander scale. Take the recent case of the F-22 Raptor, a so-called fifth-generation fighter. As usual, costs were understated and performance exaggerated. And congressmen and women kept quiet only if the defence work was spread to their districts. Originally 650 Raptors were to be built but the production line stopped at number 182 (not including prototypes). Weapons are priced not just on airframe (often minus engines or weapons) but on the entire through-life expenses including maintenance, upgrades, training and decommissioning (which in the case of nuclear-powered subs can be very difficult and expensive). By taking average figures, the Raptor cost $377 million each to produce but the actual total costs were almost double that.

The Raptor is a very advanced aircraft and, when it is working, can be very impressive. But it is so expensive and often unreliable compared with the far more plentiful older jets that can dominate air space, whether defending US territory or in combat with, say, numerous Chinese jets over the South China Sea. In order to maintain its stealth capabilities, the Raptor carries fewer air-to-air missiles. Because it is so difficult and complex to maintain, even without combat losses, it offers a lower availability rate than older aircraft. So the Raptor may be technically better than the F-15s it replaced or any MiGs it might fly against, but far from *multiplying* force, instead force is *divided*. Because the new replacements are so expensive, older fighters, such as F-15Cs are kept in service for up to three times longer than they were designed to fly. The same applies to the B-2s. The Northrop Grumman Spirit was a beautifully designed stealth strategic bomber that could deploy nukes, conventional bombs or stand-off weapons. Its first flight was in July 1989. Intended to penetrate Soviet air defences during the Cold War Mark 1, it ended up working effectively in Kosovo, Iraq and Afghanistan. Originally the US Air Force was hoping to get over a hundred but the skyrocketing price of at least $2 billion (including complex maintenance etc) plus accidents, meant that only twenty came into service and only a few were usually on active duty at one time. As one expert noted, 'The B-2 was so colossally expensive to procure that at the time it was calculated that an aircraft of the same weight made of solid gold would have been cheaper.'[1] Planes like the Raptor or the B-2 are no longer in production so if the US went head to head with serious military powers such as China rather than rag-tag Arab armies, then losses in combat, accidents or malfunctions would seriously deplete US power. And even with second-rate forces such as the Syrians their modern Russian-supplied air defences are respected by the Americans and the Israelis.

Another fifth-generation aircraft is the F-35, Lightning II, built by Lockheed Martin, the Joint Strike Fighter. This plane and its variants have proved to be the most expensive weapon project in history. It has been plagued with design flaws, partly because its variants have had to work with vertical, short take-off and catapult-assisted landing and take-off systems. Britain is relying on this unlucky plane to act as the aircraft for its new carriers. The UK MoD changed its mind a number of times about which version it wanted – partly because the carriers had not been designed to work with all variants. By 2014 the JSF system was $163 billion over budget and seven years late. Not only Britain but a number of other US allies had invested in the project. Just like the banks after 2007, when the doctrine of 'moral hazard' was applied, some things are just politically 'too big to kill'. In July 2016 the USAF finally announced that the F-35A was in squadron service. Britain is set to pay £105 million for each plane. By contrast the trusty Harriers cost £38.6 million in 2009 prices when it was phased out. Britain is scheduled to buy 138 F-35s but can only do so slowly. By 2023 perhaps twenty-four planes may be on duty.

Even though the Pentagon has increased its budgets after the dip and expected 'peace dividend' following the collapse of the Soviet Union, inflation in defence costs is much higher than the inflation in the general economy. Nukes are also big-budget items. Britain has tried to ring-fence the soaring cost of the Trident nuclear deterrent replacement. The Brits make the subs and warheads but Washington sells London the Trident II D-5 missiles, each with up to five nuclear warheads. The UK deterrent consists of four boats, in the jargon SSBNs, nuclear-powered ballistic missile submarines. At least one is on patrol all the time and, if all normal communication is lost, then one of the tests to discover whether civilisation survives is to check if the BBC's flagship radio programme, *Today*, is still on air. In June 2016 HMS *Vengeance* – like the three other boats in its class, 1.5 times the size of a football pitch – was at sea off the US southern coast, after a £350 million refit in Plymouth, UK. Because the missile costs £17 million, it is tested around every four years (usually after a boat's refit) – training and testing have been cut to the bone throughout the MoD. Problems with the ageing system have occurred before but not with the reliability of the American missiles. In the June 2016 test firing – with no warhead of course – the missile veered off course and, apparently, headed for the US mainland around Florida. This could have been friendly fire in spades: it might even have hit Disneyland. Luckily, the test missiles have small explosives on board to blow up a rogue trajectory. (One would hope that actual nuclear launches can be aborted as well, though the MoD is understandably vague about that.) The American contractors, Lockheed Martin, and the MoD hushed up the launch failure, not least because the House of Commons was about to vote on the mega-expensive upgrade of Trident. It took six months for the cover-up to be exposed. It is an American system, so they will have to find out why the missile malfunctioned as it appears the British-made elements were not at fault. In short, it was unlikely that a British submariner had simply pressed the wrong button. Still, constant hollowing out of British defence, including the deterrent, posed serious questions, not least about Britain, soon out of the EU, and trying to find the £40 billion required to pay for the next generation of Trident. If Britain decides to remain as a nuclear power it could end up with a very expensive but unreliable deterrent – the worst of all possible worlds. The logical solution, which I researched and wrote about as far back as 1971, is to go for an Anglo-French solution. They both have very similar submarine flotillas. Of course the Americans would have to agree and the British military would have to ignore the age-old preference for fighting *against* the French rather than *with* them.

Better co-operation, especially with the French, would save a lot of money but since the Second World War Britain has always preferred to work with their American friends. It used to be joint development but now Britain buys off the US shelf. It puts power in the hands of Washington, of course, and it can cost more, not least with the recent 20 per cent weakening of the pound against the US dollar. It also means that Washington can have a veto on UK arms sales, not least when the Pentagon insists that only US nationals can work on some of the hardware and software (for instance, the Apache attack helicopter). Britain can still do the business; for example the Type 45 destroyers boast a world-beating radar and missile system. Yet the original order was reduced from twelve to six. And despite the £1 billion price tag per warship they have been plagued by engine problems that have caused the engines to shut down in warm seas. The new Astute-class sub costs £1.2 billion each. They have been beset by technical problems, and the London *Daily Telegraph* claimed that the entire fleet of seven attack submarines was out of action. The Royal Navy strongly denied this.

Britain's defence industry is dominated by BAE Systems, which has become increasingly Americanised. The industry also has a few smaller so-called 'prime contractors'. The old argument, which was based upon the theory of domestic competition among prime contractors, probably never did work. Not least because the British demand is too small. The result has been an effective monopoly led by BAE. The firm, which employs 33,000 workers, has been assiduously courted by both Labour and Tory administrations, not least because of local jobs let alone national security. BAE and Rolls Royce are set to win the £41 billion contract for the four nuclear-powered, nuclear-armed Dreadnought submarines that are to replace the ageing current Vanguard fleet. The MoD with more hope than anticipation wants to change the habit of generations: that the Dreadnought budget will not produce very late and very overpriced subs. The recent Astute-class subs were over budget and late. The ministry has said it will pay bonuses if all is done on price and on time and charge fines if the contactors bust the budget. This has been said so many times before. This will not change even though a new watchdog, the Single Source Regulations Office, has been set up. Neither BAE nor Rolls will risk being fined out of existence, whether or not they are the culprits. And they are the only local players in town.

America has also had to upgrade the defensibility of its nukes, not least in the face of Russian sabre-rattling and direct nuclear threats from rogue states such as North Korea. Pyongyang had an estimated eight warheads in January 2017 while the UK had 215. Russia could boast 7,000 compared with America's 6,800. These are estimates; warheads vary in size, date, and whether actually deployed or instead retired and stockpiled. Calculating nukes cannot be an exact science, partly because of secrecy.

Even relatively small conventional operations, such as the 2011 war with Libya, displayed the weaknesses of British and French forces – especially as Washington officially stood back from leadership. The French could at least deploy their carrier – a semi-naked Britain had none. A British frigate sent to the North African coast apparently had just four missiles for its Sea Wolf air defence system. The Royal Air Force almost exhausted its (small) stock of Paveway bombs and Brimstone missiles – although Number 10 made a big fuss about the contributions these missiles would make. The Royal Navy used up twelve of its stock of sixty-four Tomahawk cruise missiles. The US was forced to play a much bigger role than Barack Obama had planned, not just in intelligence support but also in replenishing its allies' stocks of advanced American weaponry. Britain and France were embarrassed politically and militarily by the Libyan fiasco. It ended disastrously with anarchy and jihadist advances. It also showed that the Anglo-French core of NATO didn't have adequate logistics – even with the Americans holding their hands behind the scenes.

Germany and Spain were partners in the Typhoon procurement – the Eurofighter. Despite its cost overruns – and the usual quarrels with the French, the Germans, Italians, Spanish and RAF got the multi-role combat aircraft into service. The Italians and British used it for the first time in combat in the Libyan campaign for reconnaissance and ground strikes. Ironically, this plane was well suited for Cold War Mark 2 dogfights – it was originally designed for aerial combat in the first Cold War. Despite their famed efficiency, the Germans generally managed to get less than half of their 100-odd Typhoons combat ready. The figure for the *mañana* Spanish? They usually struggled to have around five or six at two airfields ready for immediate interception. The rest of their planes were what the RAF calls 'hangar queens'. The British can generally muster maybe a few dozen for immediate interception, although if the air war continues in Syria and more Typhoons are despatched to Eastern Europe, homeland defence may be sorely tested. Asylum-seekers hijacked an Ethiopian aircraft in 2014 and landed unescorted in Geneva without any interception because the Swiss air force does not fly at weekends. So the lack of combat readiness is relevant for anti-terrorism as well as constant Russian air operations around Britain plus the northern and eastern flanks of NATO. The continuous naval patrols to curb the massive waves of unseaworthy boats crossing from North Africa also stretched NATO resources, previously strained by anti-piracy patrols in the Indian Ocean.

The 'wars of choice' in the Middle East persuaded most European members of NATO that the financial and political costs were too high and so were the casualties. Compared with major conflicts in the past, European casualties in Helmand and Iraq were small, however. Conscription has largely ended (though in some cases it is being re-introduced, for example Lithuania); families are much smaller and Europeans have become couch potatoes compared with the sufferings their forebears had to endure in the trenches. Gadget-cosseted Millennials, besides being obsessed with their phones, are also far less deferential to military and political commanders who might send these young men and women to die in foreign fields.

It may be that, just as Professor Kennedy predicted, great nations take turns to have their time in the sun. Britain's empire had a good run. The American twentieth century – running perhaps from 1918 to 2017 – was a period of US parity briefly, dominance usually and as a hyper-power monopoly, also briefly. The American Century is now over. The US carrier groups have always been the prime totem of combat power but they are ageing and increasingly vulnerable. The Americans do not head the league tables in nukes, tanks or manpower. Protected by its oceans, it is not surprising that the US has concentrated on maritime power. Equally, the Russians and Chinese, as land powers, focused initially on their armies. The Russians and Chinese have reduced and professionalised their big armies and extended their reach in the air, at sea and in space and cyber space.

As Edward Snowden revealed, the US had not been niggardly in its spending on intelligence, especially surveillance. Along with GCHQ in Cheltenham, England, the Anglo-Americans have developed a lead in cyber-sleuthing. Technically, the advances were billed as defensive, against terrorists and especially the Islamic State's skilful deployment of social media. The Americans, in cooperation with the Israelis, have also pioneered offensive cyber warfare. The well-known Stuxnet attacks on Iranian nuclear plants were just the thin edge of the wedge. The Israelis could have completely closed down Iran. And yet the Russians and Chinese and vengeful Iranians, as well as non-state actors, have proved they can do similar damage to the West. Unlike the many arms controls agreements that restrict WMD, nobody has yet begun to organise international regulations for the rapidly growing tentacles of cyber war. It is like the old Wild West but without a sheriff in sight.

The Treaty of Westphalia in 1648 introduced a novel paradigm to warfare between nations. That was a European-only deal. Munich 1938 was the last time that European powers tried to decide on war and peace without the Russians or Americans. In 1945 the atomic age ushered in new protocols. The USA is still, thank God, the only country in the world to have used nuclear weapons in anger. It was fitting that they led the many complex negotiations on arms control, including the hot lines to prevent war by accident between the superpowers. That almost happened on a few occasions. Or war by miscalculation or misinterpretation as almost happened in October 1962 in the eyeball-to-eyeball confrontation over Cuba. Economic and political power and also military influence have become more diffuse, with the weakening of Europe and the rise of China and India as well as the resurgence of Russia. Wisely, the founders of the United Nations recognised this diffusion both in its structures especially the General Assembly, while also respecting the realpolitik of the great powers that happened in time to be the first five nations to develop and test nuclear weapons.

And yet the UN has rarely managed to transcend its intrinsic limitations – the national interest of its members, big and small. Peacekeeping has assisted in some cases where great powers wanted or tolerated a neutral intervention. I have witnessed and been closely involved in too many examples of well-intentioned but failed peacekeeping or peace enforcement in Lebanon, the Balkans and most recently the biggest-ever deployment of UN forces, in Africa: in Darfur, South Sudan and the Congo. It is like a return to the Garden of Eden when Adam proposed to Eve and she hesitated. So Adam asks, 'Is there someone else?' Often – at midnight, as massacres loom, and exhausted diplomats are at the end of their tethers – the UN is the only alternative. It is rarely a permanent or good solution as, in many cases, UN forces just freeze a complex situation that could have been better resolved by allowing the conflicts to continue and thus reach a conclusion, good or bad. And the bad could be genocide again. That is a cynical approach but perhaps the world will now need more Henry Kissingers in reserve. The German-American professor did his initial academic research on the balance of power in nineteenth-century Europe. Putin has clearly returned to nineteenth-century spheres of influence and power politics. China is doing the same, not least in flexing its naval muscles and also confronting the old enemy, Japan. The nineteenth century was not entirely dictated by the law of the jungle, although in the twentieth century Hitler interpreted European politics as Darwinian struggles of the fittest.

The old rules have been torn up. David Cameron tried to adapt British national interest in an age of austerity, and Donald Trump has more than magnified this approach. In the end, Kennedy's analysis of the connection between military, especially naval power, and the domestic economy has proved true. The Western solution to the long and continuing financial crisis, mainly QE, quantitative easing, has always in the past proved catastrophic. In a simple economy, such as Zimbabwe, printing money on a grand scale inevitably produced inflation and the almost total collapse of the currency. Any first-year economics student at one of the worst British ex-polytechnics-turned-universities could explain that to Robert Mugabe. And yet Robert Mugabe earned eight degrees including two in economics. So, with this expert in charge, Zimbabwe is now one of the very few independent countries that does not have its own currency. The West is currently broke and China owns most of the public debt of the USA. It is clearly not in Beijing's interest to collapse the dollar but it does give the Chinese Communist Party massive opportunities for manipulation. It knocks the much-trumpeted but unproven Russian potential blackmail about golden showers and prostitutes during the 2016 US presidential elections into the gutter, where it belongs

The decline of the West has been a long time coming but it is no surprise that the American Century should give way to fresh political structures. Just as Margaret Thatcher refused to accept that she was supposed to manage decline but instead she reversed Britain's slide, admittedly at some social cost. President Trump said he would 'make America great again', as well as improving the social and economic conditions of his supporters. A big task. Trump, for good and evil, is still recognised as the most powerful man in the world. America has suffered a relative decline but its military power is still just about pre-eminent, though its economic base is weakening. I have listed some of the more egregious stories of defence procurement cock-ups but I could just as easily recount the same with rust-bucket tales of Russian weapons' development and the massive corruption that envelops the state direction of Chinese defence industries. The West still leads in many areas; that is why so many Chinese and Russians – let alone millions of Muslims – want to settle in North America and Western Europe. As we shall see when we look at the Islamist threat in detail, the West has been the partial cause of much of the chronic anarchy in the Arab world but it must also be understood that Arab leaders have done a good job of creating chaos all by themselves. Jihadism is fundamentally a Muslim problem so it is wrong to lay all the blame on the West. And despite the long history of predictions of Western decline, it may be wrong for Westerners to be too pessimistic. So let's emulate Monty Python's infamous song in *The Life of Brian*: 'Always look on the Bright Side of Life'.

Chapter 3

'Always Look on the Bright Side of Life'

All this talk of decline can be very depressing but there is another way of looking at life in the West. Harold Macmillan, the British prime minister, famously said told his electorate in 1957: 'You've never had it so good.' Many voters agreed with him. Britain was emerging from wartime austerity, rationing had ended and people could buy new clothes with the disposable income they now had. They probably had lavatories *inside* the house. Many owned washing machines and televisions, and maybe even fridges and phones. Central heating was rare but a minority could aspire to buying a car on the 'never-never'. Compared with 1945, life in Britain in 1957 was better, even though they worked much longer hours than they do today, and the country was rapidly losing its empire. In 1945 London ruled a quarter of the globe. Thirty years later it ran just a few small islands. It is against union rules to praise the former empire so let me quote one of the wisest of international scholars, Yuval Noah Harari:

> …in most places they accepted the end of empire with a sigh rather than a temper tantrum. They focused their efforts not on retaining power, but on transferring it as smoothly as possible. At least some of the praise usually heaped on Mahatma Gandhi for his non-violent creed is actually owed to the British Empire. Despite many years of bitter and often violent struggle, when the end of the Raj came, the Indians did not have to fight the British on the streets of Delhi and Calcutta.[1]

The empire became a voluntary Commonwealth. Unlike the French who had suffered the double humiliation of defeat and occupation in the Second

World War, and then the trauma of imperial defeats in South East Asia and Algeria, post-imperial Britons felt optimistic about the future.[2] And British premiers still deluded themselves that the UK was one of the Big Three, alongside the Soviet Union and America. So measures of prosperity and even happiness are relative and may be distinct from the decline of political power – for most people most of the time.

Earlier in the book I looked at 2016 as the *annus horribilis*. It was a wrist-slashingly depressing year for many of the *bien-pensants* in the West. Instead, it could be seen as the best year in human history. How so?

Humans appear to be hard-wired to look back to a golden age, often to a period when they were young. Then you see in the world what you carry in your heart. Lamentations of a fall from Eden have a long intellectual pedigree. The good old days were terrible, however. Nevertheless, the hunter gatherer inside us looks nervously at the horizon; fear and worry are our naked ape's tools for survival. As people get older – the mature generations tend to be more pessimistic – we can mistake negative changes in ourselves for changes in the outside world. Frankly, as we personally begin to fall apart we displace our declining condition onto our society. The once hippy and happy baby boomers now look on a consumer-rich dangerous planet about to be swamped by global warming. They forget about their former pothead behaviour and comment on how awfully rude their grandchildren are when they can be bothered to stop chasing Pokemon or whatever on their phones. In the era of global media, bad news travels much faster than good news. If it bleeds it leads, so tragic news will always top the agenda. To quote Harari again:

> Most people don't appreciate how peaceful an era we live in. None of us was alive a thousand years ago, so we easily forget how much more violent the world used to be. And as wars become more rare they attract more attention. Many more people think about the wars raging today in Afghanistan and Iraq than about the peace in which most Brazilians and Indians live.[3]

For nearly the whole planet, the golden age is *now,* not fifty years ago. We really have never had it so good. A few hundred years ago in Britain the average life expectancy was around thirty. Today it is eighty-two and increasing, it's eighty-three in Japan but around seventy-nine in the USA. For millennia, life was literally nasty, brutish and short. Until modern times, teeth were extracted by pliers and operations conducted with saws and without anaesthetics by your barber. Gibbets used to display corpses. Just thirty years ago nine out of ten Chinese lived in extreme poverty, now it is one in ten. Thirty odd years ago, half of the world's population did not have access to safe water, now over 90 per cent do. It is true that food banks have mushroomed in Britain but worldwide poverty, malnutrition, illiteracy and infant mortality are falling faster than any time in our recorded history. And despite CNN reports and Internet alarms, the world is safer. A quarter of a century ago under half the world lived under democratic governance, now perhaps two-thirds can be described as democracies. Despite the head-chopping in the Islamic State and barrel-bomb rolling in Syria, the risk of being caught up in a war is much smaller than ever. Europeans run a thirty times bigger risk of being killed by a 'normal' murderer rather than by an Islamist madman. We forget how many big wars have ended: Colombia, Angola and Sri Lanka to take just three prominent recent cases. Conflicts that the world thought unsolvable – Northern Ireland and South Africa for example – have found a sort of peace.

Take British military operations. After 1945 UK troops were killed in action every year except 1968, just before the British army was deployed in large numbers to contain the Troubles in Northern Ireland. The casualties soon mounted; 1,441 were killed in the province from 1969 to 2007. In Afghanistan, from 2001 to the end of 2015, 456 British military personnel were killed; 178 were killed in Iraq from 2003 to 2011. In the Balkans seventy-two members of the British armed forces were killed. In 1982, 237 perished in the Falklands. At the beginning of 2017, 4,500 British servicemen and women were taking part in twenty-five operations in nearly thirty countries. Yet in our so-called *annus horribilis,* 2016, not a *single* Brit was killed in action.

Since the Cold War ended, world poverty has declined from 37 per cent to 9.6 of the population. And this has not necessarily been at the expense of the West. Donald Trump talked of 'carnage' in America in his inaugural speech; since 1970 median income for low and middle-income US households has increased by 30 per cent. Add in ten years of life expectancy, plus immeasurables such as cleaner water and air, the Internet and mass entertainment and the conclusion is that, typically, President Trump was overstating his case.

Even on the environment, despite the obvious dangers of global warming and the extinction of some species, it is possible to argue that modern technology is helping to mitigate some of the effects of man's selfish behaviour; that as we get richer we get cleaner and greener. For example, despite some highly litigated exceptions, on average the quantity of oil despoiling our oceans has decreased by over 90 per cent since 1970. The Amazon habitat has been depleted but forests have re-appeared in India and even China.

The year 2016 was supposed to have been a year of hate (compared, say, with the year of love, 1967). No doubt worrying examples of anti-Semitism and Islamophobia have occurred recently in the UK but the days of racist chants at football matches are a distant memory. Hard right-wing anti-immigration parties may be blooming on the European mainland, yet their parallels in England – the British National Party and the English Defence League – have declined dramatically, partly because of lack of interest and perhaps because of the success of the more moderate UK Independence Party. A Muslim peer, Lady Warsi, said that it had become 'socially acceptable' to despise Muslims. And yet in the biggest ever single vote for any British politician, over one million Londoners voted for Muslim Sadiq Khan to become mayor in May 2016.

Most of us feel bewildered sometimes – or even most of the time – by the speed of change; the 'ask-a-five-year-old-to-programme-your-electronic-gadget' syndrome. The accelerations in technological advancement, globalisation and climate change 'have reordered the planet from top to bottom'. That was the conclusion of Thomas Friedman's influential book *Thank you for Being Late: An Optimist's Guide to Thriving in the Age of Accelerations*. It was also published in that famous year of 2016. Friedman maintained that the prime threat to health is not cancer, nor heart disease. The greatest pathology is *isolation*. 'We are the most technologically connected generation in human history – and yet more people feel isolated than ever,' argued Friedman. The connections that matter most are in the shortest supply today – human-to-human connections. More and more families are texting each other even when they are together in the same house, or even the same room. This is insane.

Friedman and others, especially Steven Pinker, revived the meliorist school, based on data, not mindless optimism. Clearly we do not live in a perfect world, though the optimists argue we live in a perfectible one. History shows that, over the long run, we have collectively made progress work.[4] Steven Pinker, a professor at Harvard, blindsided conventional thinking by demonstrating that violence in human society has dropped markedly and that we now live in the most peaceful and safe times ever. His analysis, based on extensive data, was published in 2011 under the title of *The Better Angels of our Nature*. The title comes of course from Abraham Lincoln's first inaugural address. Pinker explained convincingly how we are now living in the most peaceable era our species has known. If you lived in what Pinker described as the 'pre-state era', you had a one in six chance of dying in violent conflict. In the twentieth century, for all its military cataclysms, that number fell to 3 per cent. Between 500,000 and 900,000 people died in battle in 1950. Pinker says that by 2008 the number was down to 30,000. Inter-state and civil wars have also dramatically declined. The threats from the Islamic State today are very real but statistically the chances of being killed are much smaller than the previous risk of thermonuclear war in the Cold War and during the first and second world wars. Psychologically, however, now the threats to the West *seem* greater. But the Nazis – by all indices – were much more of an existential threat not just to Jews, gypsies and gays, but to your average man on the Clapham omnibus in Britain.

Part of the reason for more peace is that the majority of the world's population lives in democracies (around 4.1 billion) compared with 1.7 billion who are citizens of autocracies. Despite the population growth, Gross Domestic Product (GDP) per capita is much higher especially after globalisation kicked in about fifty years ago. Nine out of ten people, argued Pinker, can now read. In 1970 only 6 per cent of the planet's inhabitants owned a landline phone. By 2017 more mobiles existed than people. OK, lots of hassles come not just from obsessive phone usage (especially in quiet carriages on trains) but also other aspects of globalisation, not least the rise of robots. Many, if not most, blue-collar jobs will be automated soon. Yet this also means less backbreaking work, short working hours and longer work lives. Older people – past the former retirement age of 60 in the West – are likely to be valued for their wisdom and technical skills. Cancer will be beaten and longer lives may well be healthier lives compared with a generation or two before. Even 1957.

Friedman talked about accelerating trends. It is also possible to argue that progress is inexorably accelerating too. Some psychological coping mechanisms are needed but realism equals optimism. The lead up to the 1914 war was a disastrous accidental game of chicken that went crazily adrift and the late 1930s was about appeasement and failure to confront the evil of Nazism. As Pinker said so succinctly of his angels: we should 'reframe violence as a problem to be solved rather than a contest to be won'.

****

It is true that the Monty Python stars in the *Life of Brian* indulged in gallows humour by singing their unduly optimistic song 'Always Look on the Bright Side of Life'. They were about to die in Rome's Palestinian imperium. Today, most Westerners are pessimistic despite living in a golden era. I want to now look at the West's major threats and then offer some possibly optimistic resolutions.

Chapter 4

Where did the Islamic State come from?

From Allah, is the straightforward answer if you are a devout Islamist. The astoundingly rapid conquests by Arab forces after the death of Muhammad in 632 persuaded the faithful that God was on their side. Except for their mobility at night fighting (and new faith), Arab horsemen had no advantages over the far more powerful and technologically advanced armies of the superpowers of the day: the Byzantine and Persian empires. The small Arab armies swept from Arabia into Syria, Egypt and Mesopotamia; the Muslim forces grew bigger and expanded into central France and into India and in just over 100 years created an empire that dwarfed the Roman dominion at its peak. (I have examined this phenomenon in detail in my recent book, *The Jihadist Threat.*) Although the Muslim religion and culture remained dominant in North Africa and the Middle East, Christendom eventually fought back to overcome the Islamic military threat to Europe, especially with the dismemberment of the Ottoman caliphate at the end of the Great War. Today only a tiny piece of mainland Europe remains in the hands of the Turks.

In 2014 the establishment of a new caliphate in Syria and Iraq catapulted the Islamist project back to the epicentre of world politics. As in the era of the Prophet, the Islamic State (IS) initially swept all before it and it seemed as if Allah were blessing the *Reconquista* of the world. The Islamic State promised to take back all the previously held territories, including those in Europe. The Muslim threat to the West, both Europe and America, was put at the top of President Trump's agenda. The Donald promised to 'wipe the Islamic State from the face of the earth'. At the same time the new populism in Europe was encouraged by the Trump administration. Geert Wilders, a right-wing Dutch politician who also sported a 'bigly' blonde hairstyle, talked of Europe's collapse and warned that it was being transformed into 'Eurabia', not least by mass immigration.

A decade before, the term 'Eurabia' was popularised by Bat Ye'or (a pen name for Gisèle Littman); the Jewish writer also prophesied the return of the caliphate. Bat Ye'or fled from Egypt just after the 1956 Suez crisis and in exile became a prolific author who spent her life trying to explain the role of Christians and Jews in Muslim-dominated society. Because she had never held a formal university position, other academics tended to be very sniffy about her output. She was a scholarly polemicist but a polemicist nonetheless. She developed, some say corrupted, the Islamic concept of the proper treatment of compliant infidels under Sharia law. Bat Ye'or coined the word 'dhimmitude', loosely translated as servitude. She has been accused of creating a racist Arab-European conspiracy theory that is just as virulent as anti-Jewish conspiracies such as the forged Protocols of the Elders of Zion. Some condemn Bat Ye'or's writing as 'hate speech' on a par with Holocaust denial. Her views, however, have been influential.

Anders Behring Breivik, the Norwegian mass murderer, quoted Bat Ye'or extensively in his heavily plagiarised writings and manifesto. Breivik blamed *inter alia* Islamism and feminism for the decline of the West, while praising the monoculturalism of Japan. The media described Breivik as a white nationalist in that he was as obsessed by race as much as religion and cultural factors that were forging Eurabia. He described himself as a modern-day crusader and claimed membership of a secret Knights Templar organisation; he also claimed to worship Odin. The Norwegian psychopath also said he admired both Vladimirs: Putin and the Impaler.

Another influence on Breivik, according to his own account, was American cultural critic Bruce Bawer. His book, *While Europe Slept: How Radical Islam is Destroying the West from Within*, appeared in 2006. Once established in Western European nations, Bawer argued, Muslims avoid integration and answer only to Sharia law, while avoiding the legal systems of their host nations, at the same time encouraging the abuse of women and gays, as well as Jews and other non-Muslims. In his conclusion to this book, Bawer stated that rising birth-rates among Muslims and their refusal to integrate would allow them to dominate European society within thirty years; the only way to avoid such a disaster, he wrote, was to abolish the politically correct and multicultural doctrines that permeated the continent.

Bat Ye'or's work also influenced the popular novelist and poet Michel Houellebecq. Born on the sensual French island of Réunion in 1956, the angry young man became something of a pop-star intellectual, elevated in the only Western country which would routinely lionise poets and philosophers. American critics generally disliked his novels, calling them at best pamphlet literature and at worst pornography. Foreign literary critics had a field day but the author coolly replied: 'After two or three novels, a writer can't expect to be read. The critics have made up their minds.' In 2015 – coincidentally at the same time as the *Charlie Hebdo* massacres in Paris – Houellebecq's *Submission (Soumission* in the original French) was published. Islam of course means submission (to Allah). The novel had a big impact in France, and even generally anti-philosophical Britain. The book imagines an Islamic-dominated French coalition which came to power to prevent the victory of the right-wing Front National. The country is transformed: women are veiled, polygamy is encouraged and Sharia is imposed. Even if one dislikes the theme, it is difficult to argue with the power of the work. 'Reading Houellebecq is like being caught up in a tropical storm,' opined the London *Observer.* Many, not just Muslims, objected to his storms. The novelist survived a series of court cases in France accusing him of hate speech. He argued that he hated Islam but not individual Muslims.

The fear of Muslims taking over Europe became a part of popular consciousness – perhaps even culture – in the West, whether it was transmitted via mainstream politicians of the right, French intellectuals or mass murderers. Even films played a part. Alfonso Cuarón's powerful movie *Children of Men* portrayed a dysfunctional Britain around the year 2027. Nothing goes out of date more quickly than a film about the future. This bleak film, starring Nicholas Owen and Julianne Moore, was made in 2006, yet still rings true. It is a childless future in a dictatorship in which refugees are locked in cages and parts of Britain appear to be in the grip of civil war with asylum seekers, many of them apparently Muslim. Islamist flags flutter everywhere in the besieged urban landscape. The Mexican director certainly has flair – witness his bravura display of magic in his version of Harry Potter and also his award-winning *Gravity*. Like the novel by P.D. James, upon which the film is based, a child is finally born into the grimy dystopian world. Pregnant with all sorts of meaning, the film asks many questions and provides few answers. Are the largely Muslim immigrants responsible for the dystopia? And if no child has been born for decades to the ageing local population, wouldn't they welcome immigrants if only to provide young workers for the greying society?

****

Islamists themselves explain jihadism by going back to the roots of their faith, especially the 'pious fathers'. Fundamentalist Muslims believe that if they can re-create the moral lifestyle of the Prophet and his immediate followers then once more Allah will bless the faithful. Despite modernity, strictly following the dress and behaviour of the Prophet's times will encourage God to smile down again on His people and the true caliphate will be restored before the End Days. Before those days descend on us, shall we go back to that period to explain today's trends?

Muslims claim that Islam is a religion of peace but Muhammad led or commanded twenty-seven military campaigns and raids in ten years. Sometimes those who defied him were beheaded. A year after his death in 632 his followers were inspired to conquer Syria. A year later the Muslim armies started to conquer Iraq. In 637 the Muslim conquistadors hammered the Persians and sacked their capital. In 638 Jerusalem fell. Soon Muslim armies marched into India and Afghanistan as well as controlling Egypt and penetrating Sudan. North Africa was conquered and in 674 the Christian Byzantine capital of Constantinople was besieged for the first of many times. Soon Muslim armies moved into the southern Caucasus. After the conquest of Spain and parts of south-western France, the Saracens, as the Muslims were called in Europe, were stopped by Charles Martel in central France, which is conventionally called 'the Battle of Tours'. Different types of Islamic imperial power were to wax and wane but the later Ottoman version threatened three times the heart of Europe – by almost taking Vienna.

From a Western perspective – certainly until the Crusades – the Muslims appeared to be aggressive religious imperialists. The Prophet was recorded as saying:

> Do not look for a fight with the enemy. Beg God for peace and security. But if you do end up facing the enemy, then show endurance, and remember the gates of Paradise lie in the shadow of the sword.

Islamic scholars have debated endlessly the central concept of holy war – jihad. It can mean both an internal spiritual struggle as well as violent external conflict. If it is defined as a physical battle, should jihad be deployed defensively or offensively to protect/expand the frontiers of Islam? And is jihad an obligation for *all* Muslims? The Koran and the Prophet's sayings (*Hadith*) have been re-interpreted and re-translated as often as the Bible. Contemporary records of Muhammad are even scarcer than those of Jesus Christ. Indeed, they are practically non-existent. Arabs are not famed for their rhetorical reticence, in prose or poetry, especially after conquering the known world, so it is very strange that no single Muslim record of the age of the Prophet exists – except for two fragments, one of papyrus and the other vellum. At the same time in the wilds of northern Britain the savage Northumbrians were, *inter alia*, preserving the words of the Venerable Bede in numerous books; he was arguably the greatest of English historians. Another eminent historian, Tom Holland, writing today, said of the Prophet: 'Why not a single Arab account of his life, nor of his followers' conquests, nor of the progress of his religion from the whole of the near two centuries that followed his death?'[1]

Initially, submissive Jews and Christians were treated reasonably as 'people of the Book'. And yet within a few years of the Prophet's death, these same infidels were expelled from the whole of the Arabian peninsula. The next step was to conquer the two neighbouring superpowers: the Byzantine and Persian empires. This was approximately the view of al-Qaeda in the late 1980s. Russia had been defeated in Afghanistan and the next superpower to be targeted was America. Although we are jumping ahead of our story by 1,400 years it is important to remember the continuity and resilience of the Islamist project.

Two centuries after the Prophet's death Rome itself was sacked by Muslim armies. The Byzantine and Persian empires had recently fought each other to a standstill and corruption and plague had almost finished them off, so the Arabs advanced easily in most cases; their generalship was often impressive and, unlike the Byzantines, their armies didn't usually indulge in mutinies. And yet the Koran had not specified how the successors of the Prophet were to emerge. The descendants of Muhammad and his close followers fought over the succession and this was part cause of the endless schism within Islam between the Sunni and Shia. Despite the internal feuds over leadership, the conquests were amazing, considering the size of the invading forces. A good guess is that the army that conquered Syria was never more than 30,000 men while the initial Muslim army that marched into Egypt was probably no larger than 4,000 men.[2] Faith, mobility, the desire for booty, able tribal leadership and clever divide-and-rule tactics created an empire that ran 4,000 miles from Morocco to India; the Roman Empire was smaller – around 3,000 miles from Hadrian's Wall to the Euphrates.

Unlike the Mongol hordes, the Arabs generally imposed comparatively easy terms on the conquered peoples who rarely rose in revolt once they were overrun. At the start the empire comprised of not more than 10 per cent Muslims. The infidels had to pay double the tax of followers of Allah. It was usually better to surrender, agree on terms and pay extra tax (which was still probably lower than the previous Byzantine taxes) rather than fight to the death. Except when they occasionally rebelled the locals were usually treated fairly and they could aspire to lower taxation and social inclusion if they converted (although they couldn't of course change their mind and return to their old faith). Under the very hierarchical and exclusive class systems of the Byzantine and Persian empires the vast majority of people were a permanently excluded underclass. Full absorption into Islam took centuries, however. Still, there was much in Islam that could be understood by vanquished Christians and to a lesser extent Jews; after all, Islam claimed it was fundamentally concerned with perfecting not destroying its monotheistic predecessors. In Hugh Kennedy's sweeping account of the Arab conquests, he concluded:

> In the final analysis, the success of the Muslim conquest was a result of the unstable and impoverished natures of the whole post-Roman world into which they came, the hardness and self-reliance of the Bedouin warriors and the inspiration and the open quality of the new religion of Islam.[3]

The Arab forces were sometimes defeated by well-organised Byzantine armies but perhaps one of the most significant defeats was at the hand of the Frank, Charles Martel. He led possibly the first regular professional army in Europe since the end of the Roman Empire. Martel recovered many of the Arab saddles and started to develop the use of stirrups to create, within five years, Christian heavy cavalry, the precursors of the traditional heavily-armoured knights on horseback. One of the lessons of Martel's victory in 732 is clear. Martel won because he adapted and turned the advancing Muslims' strategic advantage – heavy cavalry – against them. This is essentially the challenge facing western European governments today. They have to adapt and turn the Islamic State's strategic advantage, its skilful use of the Internet and social media blitzkrieg, against its creator. Otherwise, the digital invasion of Europe by a virtual caliphate will continue.

Tours was a very important battle for Christendom. Whether it was *the* decisive battle of the Crescent versus the Cross is open to debate, as even more dangerous incursions from Spain soon followed. The expanding maritime power of the Islamic empire enabled conquests along the coast of southern France. Martel's son, Pippin the Short, took up the fight and his son, Charlemagne, built the first Western empire from the ruins of the Roman imperium. Western Europe became better organised, centralised and more militarised. The Arab incursions into France were halted and eventually the *Reconquista* of the Iberian peninsula would gather momentum.

The main bulwark against the Muslim advance into the Christian West had long been the armies of the Byzantine Empire but by 1071 they had been pushed out of the fertile areas of Anatolia (in today's Turkey). The salvation of the Orthodox Christians in Constantinople was then considered to be largely in the hands of the diverse Catholic military powers in Europe and the naval strength of the Italian states, plus the key – if erratic – support of the papacy. The West, however, was mired in a similar schism to the Sunni versus Shia acrimony. Muslims had already conquered many squabbling Christian sects but the Catholic versus Greek orthodox enmity was to constantly undermine Western ramparts.

The papacy's meddling in the Byzantine Empire by sponsoring the Crusades initially buttressed the defence against Islam. In 1095 the first of a series of seven ill-co-ordinated though often savage invasions of the Holy Land (and its neighbours) began, establishing various Christian kingdoms in the Levant. Over the course of two centuries the undiscriminating Crusaders preyed on Byzantine Greeks as often as Jews, Arab Christians or Muslims. Some Christian states – locally they were called 'Franks' – allied with Saracens in battles between the small, usually squabbling and often precarious, Christian kingdoms. The great Muslim warrior Saladin (probably of Kurdish extraction) started his campaign against the crusaders in 1164 and conquered Damascus in 1174 and Jerusalem in 1187. The last Christian bastion, Acre, fell in 1291.

The crusader states had been summoned into existence in 1095 when Pope Urban II called for a rescue of the Christians allegedly being abused by the Saracens, especially when they were on pilgrimage. Many of the accusations were pure propaganda. Four main crusades followed during the 200-year adventure. Other smaller ones ensued in the Levant, as well as numerous crusades within Europe, some against so-called heretics and pagans and others against Muslims in Iberia. Despite the papal influence, no central command structure emerged for the crusades in the Levant. Christians travelled across Europe, living off the land, to reach Jerusalem for a host of reasons – penance, salvation, adventure, booty, military experience or because of feudal obligation. The fighting men (and often their women and children plus servants) were usually raised and led by lords and sometimes kings, so the Crusaders were deeply parochial and feudal in their loyalty. The lack of unified command ultimately created the conditions for their defeat by a much bigger, perhaps better-motivated and, more important, *local* enemy whose logistics chain did not ultimately depend on the poor communications with faraway Europe.

******

Hadda Street in the Yemeni capital of Sana'a used to have smart-ish restaurants and, by local standards, upmarket shops. It was 29 October 2010, long before the civil war that ravaged the Yemeni capital. The Fedex office in Hadda Street was busy; a veiled woman, whose ID said she was called Hannan al-Samawi, an engineering student, left a box for shipping to the city of Chicago, Illinois.

The box contained some traditional Yemeni clothing, a souvenir model of Yemen's tall mud buildings and a handful of books in English, including George Eliot's The Mill on the Floss. *Also inside was a Hewlett-Packard LaserJet printer; hidden in the printer were 300 grams of the industrial explosive PETN. This was more than enough to bring down a jetliner in flight. Primed to blow up over Chicago, the bomb had probably been made by a Saudi specialist working for al-Qaeda in the Arabian Peninsula. The target was supposed to be innocent Chicagoans. It was, however, addressed to an old enemy of Jihad, perhaps the most hated of all the unbelievers. It was addressed to 'Reynald Krak', a pseudonym for Reynald de Châtillon. He was highly unlikely to receive his present as he was a crusader prince who had been beheaded 823 years before.*

That modern-day jihadists should address their bomb to a long-dead Frankish knight indicates the continuity and longevity of the conflict. Secular Westerners may have a vague idea about what happened in the Crusades but to an Islamist it is all part and parcel of current oppression. Westerners might know that the Crusades into the Holy Land, as Christians called the region, were the first major counter-strikes in the Middle East to stop the civilisation of Islam that had been expanding for centuries. Islam had generated a culture that was superior in many ways, besides its fighting skills – architecture, medicine, science, mathematics, commerce and much else. The First Crusade captured Jerusalem in 1099 but the Third Crusade (1189-92) is probably the best remembered in Europe because of its leading man, Richard the Lionheart. Apart from popular films such as Ridley Scott's The Kingdom of Heaven *few now recall these swashbuckling events. To many Muslims the Islamic world is still engaged in both a virtual and virtuous real war against the crusader onslaught. Any loss of Islamic territory, in Al-Andalus in Spain or to Reynald de Châtillon in the Levant or to Zionist occupation in Palestine or American-led invasion of Iraq in 2003, all form a continuum. All are crusaders. The Islamic State would even extend this definition to Western tourists in Tunisia, for example.*

Oddly, Western history has tended to accept the Muslim interpretation of Reynald's life as well as contemporary accounts by some of his Christian enemies. Recent attempts have been made to resuscitate a more positive image.⁴ His greed and aggression have been blamed for the fall of the Kingdom of Jerusalem. Yes, Reynald was tough and brutal but it was a tough and brutal age. Reynald was portrayed as a buffoonish Templar in Scott's film – he was neither. He was one of the few leaders who constantly took the fight to the enemy. He set up a small maritime force that raided in the Red Sea and it was even suggested that he would attack the holiest city of Mecca – this united all Muslims then and perhaps even now in utter loathing for the knight, who was beheaded by Saladin himself, according to some accounts.

****

Islamic growth was not achieved only at the point of a sword. A golden Islamic age was epitomised by the fourth Abbasid caliph, Harun al-Rashid (763-809). Far from focusing on the narrow confines of the Koran, Islamic scholars reached out to the ancient texts of classic antiquity of Greece and Rome as well as Persia that were translated into Arabic and thus preserved. Without this Arab scholarship Western Europe might have had no Renaissance and perhaps remained mired in the Dark Ages. Baghdad, Córdoba and Cairo became intellectual centres of learning; Islamic universities were established long before Oxbridge. The decline in Islamic cultural glory was not sudden although the 1258 sacking of Baghdad by the Mongols was a clear-cut watershed. External and internal rivalries also played a role.

From the 950s the Seljuk Turks from today's Uzbekistan started to embrace Islam and they were to become allies and opponents of the Arab-inspired empire. The Crusades and then the *Reconquista* of the Iberian peninsula by 1492 undermined Islamic confidence, though the Mongol hordes did the most damage. The Mongols destroyed nearly all they could not carry back to the steppes. The destruction of mosques and libraries is the main reason for the lack of records of the first centuries of Muhammad's message from God, or so many of my Muslim academic friends keep telling me. The Islamic world never fully recovered from the Mongol devastation, although the ideal of a jihadist empire did not die.

It found new meaning in the Ottoman Empire. The term 'Ottoman' comes from the anglicisation of Osman I, the founder of the Ottoman dynasty. Nomadic horsemen from Turkmenistan, displaced by Mongol invasions, rode into Anatolia to aid the Seljuks of Rum in their conflict with the Byzantines. Osman I (1258-1326) extended what became known as 'Turkish' settlement and thus sparked an Islamic empire that endured for 600 years. Like the earlier Arab nomadic armies, the Turks relied on conquest, plunder and slavery – sometimes in the name of jihad – to control North Africa, the Middle East and much of south-eastern Europe. Warfare with the Christian West was continuous but sporadic in intensity and alliances. Sometimes the French, for example, allied with the Turks to defeat their Christian rivals, especially the Habsburgs. The Ottomans defeated Serb Christian forces in Kosovo in 1389 which led to the rapid penetration of Muslim forces into Europe. In what is sometimes described as the last crusader counter-offensive, at the Battle of Nicopolis on the Danube in September 1389, a coalition of Christian armies was thrashed, partly because of poor preparation and the drunken arrogance of some French knights. After this humiliating defeat the European heartland stood almost defenceless against the Ottoman onslaught.

The apex of Christian humiliation was the catastrophic fall of Constantinople in 1453. The city had been besieged many times, though usually naval power from the Italian republics or Christian armies from the Balkans had saved the sclerotic Byzantine Empire that had been reduced almost to the size of a city-state surrounded by hostile forces. Its other major possessions and forces were in Greece. The last Byzantine emperor, Constantine XI, fought hard on sea, land and in underground tunnels against the Islamic armies, led by Sultan Mehmed II, which outnumbered the defenders by ten to one. Some of the defenders were Turks, just as Christian troops (and slaves) fought for the sultan, who used highly paid Christian engineers to build his super-sized cannon.

It had been the dream of Islamic rulers for centuries to conquer the new Rome. This was a far greater blow than the fall of Jerusalem and then all the Holy Land more than two centuries before. Constantinople became Istanbul and the heart of the Ottoman caliphate. The exquisite patriarchal basilica of Hagia Sophia was transformed into a mosque. The Muslim empire now controlled the major overland routes between Europe and Asia. The caliphate's armies and navies were modernised under a series of capable warrior sultans. The Ottoman dominion expanded even further in the fifteenth and sixteenth centuries; Persia and Egypt, for example, were taken back into the caliph's hands.

****

The fall of Constantinople – like the fall of Jerusalem – led to much soul-searching in the West. The papacy called for a renewed crusade but Europe was too exhausted by its own internal wars. The Hundred Years' War had ended in the same year as the Ottoman triumph over the Byzantines and the knights of England and France were exhausted by internecine Christian warfare. Farther east, the Greek-Latin religious divide was as instrumental in the Byzantine Empire's demise as the aggression of the Muslim armies. Then, in the next century, Europe became even more bisected by religion: the Reformation and the Counter-Reformation. The papacy's calls for Christendom to retake the lands lost to Islam fell on deaf ears. One empire, however, could not disengage from the rise of Ottoman militarism: the great maritime power of Venice. A few years after the humiliation of Constantinople, Giacomo de'Languschi, a Venetian visitor of the now Muslim-dominated city, described the young Ottoman conqueror in chilling terms:

The sovereign, the Grand Turk Mehmet Bey, is a youth of twenty-six, well-built, of large rather than medium stature, expert at arms, of aspect more frightening than venerable, laughing seldom, full of circumspection, endowed with great generosity, obstinate in pursuing his plans, bold in all undertakings, as eager for fame as Alexander of Macedonia. Daily he has Roman and other historical works read to him by a companion called Ciriaco of Ancona and another Italian... . He speaks three languages, Turkish, Greek and Slavic. He is at great pains to learn the geography of Italy and to inform himself... where the seat of the pope is and that of the emperor, and how many kingdoms there are in

Europe. He possesses a map of Europe with the countries and provinces. He learns nothing with greater interest and enthusiasm than the geography of the world and military affairs; he burns with desire to dominate; he is a shrewd investigator of conditions. It is with such a man that we Christians have to deal. Today, he says, the times have changed, and declares that he will advance from east to west as in former times the westerners advanced into the Orient. There must, he says, be only one, one faith, and one sovereignty in the world.[5]

The Sultan's ambition was to invade Italy and be crowned in Rome, just like Caesar. Immediately after the fall of Constantinople, Venice began to fortify its many distant islands and colonies. Often the boundaries of war and peace were blurred, just as modern-day Islamist terrorism falls short of formal war. For example, unattributed mounted raiders nibbled at frontier zones until territory was softened up for open war, or 'freelance' pirates ransacked islands. Meanwhile waves of immigrants, mainly Greeks, flooded the frontier territories. Besides the 'unofficial' destabilisation, a cold war of smoke and mirrors characterised Venetian-Ottoman relations. Spies proliferated on both sides, as well as disinformation, torture, assassination and acts of sabotage. It was the patriotic duty of every Venetian merchant to spy for his homeland. Bribery was rampant and often Jewish professionals were deployed as middlemen because it was assumed they were more neutral in Christian-Muslim negotiations. In 1456, for example, the sultan's Jewish doctor was paid 1,000 ducats by Venice to smooth difficulties over the islands of Imbros and Lemnos. Endless conspiracies ensued – fixing the 'sultan problem' with a single phial was always attractive to scheming doges.

No matter what the papacy did, Venice was too busy fighting its Italian neighbours, especially Milan and Florence, and trying to placate the Turks, to lead an effective combined Christian European navy. Venice did see itself as a front-line state, the 'shield of Christendom', but other Christian powers considered the maritime empire as too avaricious and in the infidels' pockets. And yet all the Italian city states did deals with the caliphate when it suited them. The King of Naples was willing to open his ports to the sultan's ships for the right price. Venice was well aware that its many rivals wanted nothing better than to see it exhaust its treasure in fighting a long and bitter war with the Ottomans. Even when popes were so inclined, none could persuade the Christian powers to unite to retrieve Constantinople, let alone Jerusalem. Soon the focus was on defending heartland Vienna, not an offensive in the Levant. In the decades after the Islamicisation of the Christian citadel of Constantinople, Europe was too divided, too secular and too materialistic to heed any papal bull to replay the golden oldies of the Crusades.

In 1461 a Venetian force intercepted a ship carrying the painter and sculptor Matteo de'Pasti, who was on his way from Rimini to Istanbul to paint the sultan's portrait. They found in his possession the latest publications on military tactics and war machines and a detailed map of the Adriatic. He was travelling at the request of Sigismondo Malatesta, the co-called 'Wolf of Rimini', arguably the most treacherous and toughest of the condottieri *in Italy. A few years later the Wolf became the ally of Venice. And yet by 1503 Venice had been forced to sign a humiliating peace with the Ottomans. The proud Venetians would have to dip their flags to passing Ottoman vessels. A Venetian ambassador to the sultan's court was told here was little point in his role. 'Up till now you have married the sea,' the vizier told him, 'but from now on it's our turn. We have got more sea than you.' European merchant ships could hardly sail in the eastern Mediterranean without Turkish permission. Only a few large islands – Corfu, Crete, Cyprus and Rhodes – were left in Christian hands.*

The Turks achieved naval superiority without technical breakthroughs, fought few naval battles and won none conclusively. Their power lay in their massive army – their ships were used more for maritime, support, logistics and occasional amphibious operations. They had simply swallowed up nearly all the colonies and ports that the Venetian galleys depended on for re-supply.

Although Venice had been perhaps the early prototype of European colonisation, it was a great power based upon a fragile centre that was sinking from the start. It was free from feudalism but encased in red tape. Venice displaced the chivalric European knight with the heroic model of the master-merchant. It was the forerunner of classic capitalism – balancing supply and demand, satisfying consumer choice, with reliable and consistent laws and taxes founded on a sound currency. Holland and England took note and started their own empires, based upon the Portuguese and Spanish discoveries, especially the southern African route to the Indies. This spelled the end for Venice's role of middleman and also the Turkish monopoly of the Asian trade routes. The Ottomans had pounded away at Corfu; this was the strategic door to the Adriatic yet it had remained firmly shut to them. Venice was eventually to fall to a Christian invader when Napoleon marched into St Mark's Square and dragged the famous 'bronze' horses off to Paris in great carts. The sculptures, originally from the Second or Third Century AD, had been stolen by the Venetians during the sacking of Constantinople in 1204. So Napoleon was re-enacting internecine theft within Christendom, The horses were returned after the Battle of Waterloo in 1815 but were finally overcome by the effects of air pollution and put in safe storage in the 1980s.

******

Suleiman the Magnificent had become sultan in 1520. As his moniker suggests, he was a dynamic and charismatic ruler. This more-than-able warrior came at a time of maximum chaos in Christian Europe. A young Medici pope, Leo X, ruled in Rome. A Habsburg, Charles V, had just been crowned Holy Roman Emperor. In England Henry VIII had just married Charles's aunt, Catherine of Aragon. Worse, for Christian unity, in Germany Martin Luther was challenging the role of the pope and Catholic kings. The Reformation turmoil was a perfect time for an ambitious sultan to divide and rule; perhaps even to take back Al-Andalus. It was only on 2 January 1492 that Boabdil, the Muslim emir of Granada, surrendered the keys of his city to Ferdinand and Isabella, monarchs of the newly united Christian kingdoms of Castile and Aragon. Both Christian leaders wore resplendent Moorish costume. The defeated emir said in Arabic to Ferdinand: 'God loves you greatly, Sir, these are the keys of this paradise.' The last Muslim ruler in Spain then left for exile in North Africa. In contrast, in 1521 Suleiman led his armies out of Istanbul and marched into the heart of Europe. Belgrade and most of the kingdom of Hungary fell into Ottoman hands in the high tide of Muslim expansion into Europe. In 1529 Suleiman besieged Vienna. He was pushed back but his forces returned in 1532. If Vienna had fallen so would much of Western Christendom. The Ottomans for the time being were contained as they turned their attention east to Baghdad and the Persian Gulf.

Some military unity had been displayed in the defence of Vienna, although the more common pattern was for Istanbul to divide and rule. France and rival Habsburgs made various separate pacts with the Ottomans. Finally, the Turkish conquest of Cyprus, accompanied by massacres of Christians, temporarily united many of the quarrelsome European states; the pope forged an uneasy alliance called the Holy League. Turkish land grabs as well as threats to maritime commerce were as much inducements as the reverence for Jesus Christ. In October 1571 the Holy League managed to stop squabbling long enough to assemble a fleet in the Bay of Patmas near Lepanto. The sultan had more ships and more men, though far fewer cannon. Spanish sailors, however, ventured to capture the naval commander, Ali Pasha, on his flagship, the *Sultana*, and then displayed his head on a pike. Demoralised, the surviving Ottoman ships withdrew. Over 12,000 Christian slaves were unshackled from their oars. The European coalition lost fifty galleys and suffered 13,000 casualties. One of those wounded on board a Genoese ship was Miguel de Cervantes, who wrote *Don Quixote*, perhaps the first modern European novel. The Ottomans, however, possessed the biggest and arguably the most efficient military machine in the world, so they soon rebuilt their navy and augmented their armies. The threat to the West remained. They had to face challenges, however, in the eastern parts of their vast empire as well as rebellions in North Africa.

*****

Today it is Horse Guards Parade in central London. On 17 November 1600 it was the tiltyard of Whitehall Palace. Each year Her Majesty Queen Elizabeth celebrated the date with an ornate ceremonial entrance into London, returning from her summer residence at Windsor, Richmond or Hampton Court. A tall dark bearded man is standing aside from his retinue. He is wearing a long black robe, bright white linen turban and a huge richly decorated scimitar, a Maghreb nimcha; it is strapped to his waist – though his whole demeanour suggests that the sword could be used to kill as much as for decoration.[6] He is Abd al-Wahid bin Masoud bin Muhammad al-Annuri, the Moroccan ambassador to the court of Queen Elizabeth. He is halfway through his six-month visit to London on behalf of Mulay Ahmed al-Mansur, the Sultan of Morocco. The ambassador is in England specifically to secure a formal Anglo-Moroccan alliance against Catholic Spain, the Queen's greatest enemy. The sultan dreams of restoring Al-Andalus while the Protestant English ruler wants to undermine the Spanish in any way possible. The Moroccans even talk of co-operating against Spanish interests in the New World. For around forty years all things Moroccan and indeed Islamic had been in fashion in London, not just diplomacy, but food, furnishings, clothing and art. It was not until modern times that Islamic culture had such an influence in a Western Christian state.[7]

This year the Tilts – a pageant based upon the medieval jousting tournaments – is more ambitious than ever. The flamboyance is intended to show foreign ambassadors the new power of England, at peace with itself at home and confident abroad, now that the Spanish king, Philip II, had died two years before. England is still officially at war with Spain but the invasion threat has receded. Still, behind the scenes not all is well, not least the question of who is to succeed the 'Virgin Queen'. Elizabeth is now 67 years old, looking very worn and her teeth are black, perhaps because of all the Moroccan sugar she has consumed.

The handsome Moroccan envoy meets the Queen a number of times, and not all their words, first in Spanish, and then Italian, are recorded. The sultan offers men and equipment to launch an Anglo-Moroccan invasion of Spain. The ambitious sultan also wants London's backing against the former suzerain – the Ottoman caliph. Such an alliance would set Christian against Christian and Muslim against Muslim and all based upon a peculiar and secret Sunni-Protestant pact. Protestantism is new, remember. Most Christians loathe the slave-dealing Turks. Others, especially Protestants, are more sympathetic to Islam's refusal to worship icons and its veneration of and literal acceptance of a holy book. This is a faith with which we can do business, many diplomats and merchants averred. Tens of thousands of Europeans were forcibly converted, at the point of a sword, and became part of the army of white slaves, especially in Morocco. And yet others were attracted to the religion and converted out of choice. It was called 'turning Turk'. London's flirtation with Islam only convinced the Catholic powers that Protestant England and Muslims were two sides of the same heretical coin.

As it happened, during Elizabeth's forty-five-year reign, London made deals and treaties with Muslim kingdoms, including Morocco and the Ottoman caliphate, but also reached out to businessmen and courtiers in Syria, the Persian Gulf and Shia leaders in Persia as well as Mughal India. In 1599, for example, Queen Elizabeth sent a Lancastrian blacksmith, Thomas Dallam, to Istanbul to play his clockwork organ in front of the sultan. That was an interesting oddity but the English government also sent a number of merchants and ambassadors to the court in Istanbul as well as to the Persian shah.

Tudor fascination with the Islamic world went further back than Elizabeth. Her father, Henry VIII, used to dress up in silk and velvet, sporting a turban and scimitar 'apparelled after the Turkey fashion'. Turkish carpets and wall coverings became all the rage. Even the language was influenced; words such as sugar, as well as turquoise (Turkey stone), indigo and tulip. Zero entered the lexicon from Islamic mathematics. Literature was strongly influenced, not just books about travels in the Orient; hardly a play in the late Elizabethan period was written without a minor or major Moorish character. Marlowe's Tamburlaine *and Shakespeare's* Titus Andronicus *and* The Merchant of Venice *are the best-known examples today.*

The infatuation with Turkish style did not lead to much of religious substance – beyond fashion and realpolitik. There was little attempt to understand Islam in its own theological context. The Koran was not translated into English until 1649. Shakespeare and his contemporaries would not have recognised the term 'Muslim' – it was probably first used in English in 1615. The terms used were usually Moors, Ottomites, Saracens, Turks or various spellings of Mahometans. Many of the portrayals of Muslims in the plays were full of charming wild Turks with turbans and scimitars. Edward Alleyn, a famously stentorian actor of the time, starred in Tamburlaine; *in the second part of Marlowe's sensationally popular play written in 1587, Alleyn as Tamburlaine cursed Muhammad and then burnt the Koran on stage. This act was famously censored when the same play was performed in the London Barbican Theatre in 2005 following the Islamist transport bombings of 7 July that year.*

The London flirtation with Islam was ended when England's King James II, a Catholic, sought rapprochement with Catholic Europe. The new Stuart king suffered from delusions of grandeur; he believed his destiny was to unify Christendom. He thought he could unite Catholicism and the Greek Orthodox Church as well as reconciling with Protestantism. If these three branches of Christianity could have at least resolved their differences, then the Islamic threat would have been deterred much earlier.

*****

The failure of the Ottomans to take Vienna in 1683 marked the final push of Islamic expansion into Europe. Thereafter the empire went into decline.

In the beginning the sultans were generally capable. After Suleiman the Magnificent, well, they were not so magnificent. They were often plain incompetent or self-indulgent, more interested in decorating their palaces or frolicking in their harems rather than improving their armies or navies. Their military technology stagnated while the Western powers innovated rapidly, especially as they started to build maritime empires. The Russians expanded too and helped their Slavic Christian cousins in the Balkans. The various Christian revolts, especially the Serbs and later the Bulgarians, inspired much sympathy in the West. The best publicised fight for freedom against the Turkish overlords was in the Greece of the 1820s, immortalised by the poetry and subsequent death of Lord Byron. The European powers were nibbling to death Ottoman possessions in the Balkans; Bulgaria gained virtual independence as did Serbia and small Montenegro. Austria-Hungary annexed Bosnia-Herzegovina. At the Congress of Berlin in 1878 Britain took over Cyprus and, after 1882, displaced French influence in Egypt, nominally under Ottoman rule.[8] Turkey was considered 'the sick man of Europe' and ready to be put out of his misery.

As the caliphate shrank the Ottoman rulers turned in on themselves, not least by massacring Christian Armenians because they were accused of sympathising with the Russians. In 1908 the Young Turks' revolution tried to reform the military and politics. Nevertheless Libya was taken over by Italy and in the Balkan wars of 1912-13 Turkey lost more European territories. By the eve of the First World War the once great Muslim empire consisted of around 15 million people in modern Turkey and approximately 4 million Arab subjects in Syria, Lebanon, Palestine and Jordan, with over 2 million in Iraq. Another million Arabs were under nominal Ottoman suzerainty in the Arabian peninsula, where the whole Islamic adventure had originally begun.

Despite so many battles with the Austrians and Hungarians, the Turks joined the side of Austria-Hungary and Germany in 1914. The caliph called for jihad against his enemies but it was sometimes hard to distinguish between the merits, say, of an Austrian infidel versus a French version. Whether they fought for Allah or empire Turkish troops were hardy and generally fought well, even when poorly led. As it happened the British and French authorities took the summons to holy war more seriously than the Muslims it was aimed at, not least those Muslims in the French and British empires. The Allies got a bloody nose in the Gallipoli campaign and suffered one of Britain's most humiliating defeats at Kut in Iraq. The whole purpose of Anglo-French operations in the Middle East was to break away from the stalemate in the trenches of the Western Front by diverting manpower from the armies of the Central Powers. Turkey was seen as a soft target. So Anglo-French diversionary strategies colluded with the Arab revolt of 1916. The prime purpose of the British was to tie up Ottoman troops to prevent their advance again on British control in Egypt, especially the Suez Canal. This was not only the proverbial jugular of the empire, access to the Raj, but also to oil in Persia. The Royal Navy had largely converted to oil just before the Great War.

****

Lawrence of Arabia *was a good, even a great, film but David Lean, the director, played fast and loose with the truth. So did T.E. Lawrence in his epic book,* Seven Pillars of Wisdom. *This title was something of a joke – it was the name of his unfinished first novel that Lawrence burned. It indicates perhaps that Lawrence was more intent on writing literature than narrative factual history. He admitted the contemporary influences of Ezra Pound, W.B. Yeats and T.S. Elliot. The most dramatic episode in the book – his flogging and sodomisation in Deraa – did not and could not have happened. The dates given, for example, did not accord with his known movements. Myriads of professional scholars, and amateur psychologists and psychiatrists, have tried to explain the Deraa buggeration, though it can be better explained in terms of Greek epic literary norms not least the (necessary) suffering of the hero. One of the best analyses is Angus Calder's introduction to the 1997 edition of* Seven Pillars*:*

The epic of Homer which Lawrence chose to carry on his campaign was the Odyssey. Seven Pillars *resembles that work only in so far as its protagonist steers though great difficulties towards a goal reached at last. But Damascus is certainly not like Ithaca, not Lawrence's home and no Penelope awaits him there.* Seven Pillars *has much more in common with the* Iliad.

Thomas Edward Lawrence was undoubtedly a fascinating character, though not quite the maker of the modern Middle East. Arguably, British Arabist Gertrude Bell did more to win over Arab leaders, especially in Iraq. Bell was Lawrence's equal in every sense: the first woman to achieve a first from Oxford (in modern history), an archaeologist, Arabist, adventurer and probably a spy. Arabs knew her as 'al-Khatun', the lady, not least because she refused to dress like an Arab or Persian and instead, even on camel-back, wore fashionable Western clothes. Britain's popular media lionised her and called her 'the Queen of the Desert'. She was perhaps the most famous woman in the empire, though she is largely forgotten now, even in her native County Durham. When Bell met Lawrence at an archaeological dig at Carchemish in Mesopotamia, he said later 'she was a wonderful person, not very like a woman' – which was presumably meant as a compliment. Bell achieved a great deal in the post-war Cairo conference but hardly any of the participants chose to mention much of the desert Queen in their despatches and memoirs, even though she did more than Lawrence to secure a Hashemite king in Iraq.

A number of other British (and French) officers played significant roles in persuading some of the Arab tribal leaders that they should pursue independence from the Turks and found a unified Arab state. Colonel Lawrence was one of the most controversial warriors in recent history, although he did not have the benefit of a single day's military training. He was an academic, an aesthete and archaeologist (as well as a manic depressive) who portrayed, not least in the public eye, the British leadership of the Arab Revolt. Although Lawrence's affection for the Bedouin was not in doubt, his endeavours were totally in the framework of British imperialism. He was leading 'his' Arabs as no native could have, over hundreds of miles of desert, to achieve the Holy Grail – Lawrence was obsessed by Arthurian legends as a boy – of conquering Damascus. In fact he epitomised the concept of 'indirect rule' that the British colonials practised in much of Africa and Asia. As Angus Calder wrote: 'The wise and selfless Briton, ideally, advised a legitimate native ruler to the benefit of the latter and his people.' Lawrence would today be accused of that most heinous of Western crimes – Orientalism. Most of the Arabs fought most of the time for money, not nationalism or Allah. The locals, for example, were usually happy to sell food to Turkish garrisons. Many Bedouin, however, disliked the crucial imperial jugular, the Hejaz railway, not least because it deprived them of the lucrative job of escorting pilgrim traffic southward. And the Arabs liked the supply of guns and explosives. To be fair, most did respond well to the charismatic leadership of Lawrence, as well as his understanding of the nuances of Bedouin life. In the end, though, it was Lawrence's access to extensive supplies of British gold that swung the argument, plus attacks on trains, stations and small towns that provided lots of loot. Lawrence's account, however, unsurprisingly emphasises the nationalist inspiration of the irregulars who followed him and Prince Feisal. Lawrence may have mixed fact and fiction and suffered from a tortured inner life, not least his masochistic sexuality, but he also had the moral courage to refuse a knighthood at the very moment that George V was about to confer the honour on him, because he believed that the British government had betrayed the Arabs, he explained. Ill-timed, rude but gutsy. He also donated the considerable royalties from the popular editions of his flawed masterpiece to a Royal Air Force charity.

Lawrence appeared to be very modern in one sense – he wrote as though what is true is what people are willing to believe. And people usually believe what they want to believe in big matters such as war and empire. The Seven Pillars, *however, is more quoted than read. If one disregards Lawrence as writer, one question still remains. How did this painfully shy Oxford archaeologist without a day of formal military service become a successful battlefield commander of a revolutionary irregular army that tried to change the course of Middle East politics? As Lawrence himself implied, the great revolt was a 'sideshow of a sideshow' but it also led almost by accident to a map dictated by imperialists which has lasted intact almost to this day. Much of the region's cartography was in fact created by the British and French. During the peace conferences after the Great War, covetous colonial officials often referred to the area – among themselves – as the 'Great Loot'. 'Why is their sand covering all our oil?' they would quip.*

US President Woodrow Wilson wanted a new world order but the Paris peace conference degenerated into the usual smoke-filled backroom deals, vengeful treaties and arbitrary borders. The Great Loot, the carving up of the carcass of the Ottoman Empire, would bring little for the Arabs but a lot for the French and British empires. Lawrence had won his war though he lost his peace. He was stripped of his credentials at Paris and barred from helping old comrades in arms, especially Prince Feisal. Lawrence and Feisal did succeed, however, in reaching an understanding with the Zionists, particularly a prominent leader, Chaim Weizmann. Hashemite support for the Zionist programme was to be traded for Jewish influence in persuading the Americans to back an independent Arab Syria. Generally the Arab leaders preferred the involvement of the Americans – even control of League trusteeships, because they were considered far less grasping than the devils they already knew, the British and French.

There are many what ifs in the Lawrence story. What would the region look like today if the unified Arab nation had been won in Paris and the following peace conferences? And what would have happened if the early post-war Zionists in Palestine had been able to negotiate with Feisal Hussein who had talked of 'the racial kinship and ancient bonds' that existed between Jew and Arab? And American peacekeepers putting boots on the ground? It seems strange today to recall the Arab and Muslim worlds clamouring for American intervention in their lands.[9]

Lawrence's Arab allies received little of what they had been promised and so he retreated from public life. Winston Churchill, almost a hero-worshipper of Lawrence, and then Colonial Secretary, persuaded him to attend the 1921 Cairo conference. Churchill's patronage allowed Lawrence to be an unseen kingmaker – literally, though Gertrude Bell was also a crucial if unsung participant. Feisal, for example, was placed on the throne of a new state, Iraq. His authority in the Hejaz was also upheld. Feisal's apparently indolent son, Abdullah, was given Transjordan; later he proved a very capable leader. Palestine on the other side of the Jordan was taken over by a British Mandate under the League of Nations. Lawrence did his best for his Arab brothers but by and large his main legacy has been inadvertent. The 'porcelain peace' of the Paris conference has left a legacy of usually cruel, kleptocratic, incompetent Arab leaders and impoverished people who have been encouraged by their governments to blame Western interventions often hand in hand with Zionism for all their ills. Few Arab rulers have indulged in much self-criticism. Even the Englishman who risked all for their cause is usually castigated for his 'great betrayal'.

The worse the contemporary Arab world becomes, somehow in a strange backwash the more the earlier representatives of empire are blamed. Mark Sykes would always get a pasting. And yet somehow Lawrence was different. He was a very unusual man and every generation projects its own prejudices and fears, visions and fantasias upon this Englishman who loved the Bedouin.

******

T.E. Lawrence had promised his Arab friends much but the 1916 Sykes-Picot secret pact was largely enacted despite the modifications made at the Cairo conference. The Russians had also been involved in Sykes-Picot – looking for some of the Ottoman pie to slice up. Once the Bolsheviks took over in late 1917 they published the details of the Anglo-French conspiracy. The Turks and Arabs were furious. An exception was Feisal. The long British affair with the Hashemites, who provided the kings in Jordan and briefly in Iraq, was based upon a genuine belief that by bolstering the conservative forces of Islam and the ruling families from the ancient Bedouin tribes, the British could maintain Arab stability at least from the radical forces of secular nationalism, perhaps tinged with the Bolshevism spreading from Russia.

During the Second World War many Arabs sided with the Axis forces as the best means of booting out their colonial masters as well as curbing Zionism. The best-known pro-German Arab leader, the Grand Mufti of Jerusalem, sought exile in Nazi-occupied Europe from where, on 25 November 1941, he declared a jihad against the Allies. Hitler occasionally expressed sympathy with the Arab cause, sometimes mentioning approvingly their rapid military advance after the death of the Prophet. The Führer also shared many Arabs' hatred of the Jews. The Germans supported the Arab revolt in Palestine (1936-9) and backed a pro-Axis government in Iraq in 1941. After the fall of France in 1940, some Arabs chanted (in Arabic):

No more Monsieur
No more Mister
Allah's in heaven
And Hitler's on earth

Eminent generals such as Erwin Rommel were often feted in Arab society. The Germans formed a Muslim *Waffen* SS division and set up the Free Arabia radio station. One of those seduced by Nazi propaganda was a young Anwar Sadat, later to be president of Egypt. Some pro-Axis Arabs became involved in extensive sabotage and intelligence operations in North Africa.

There never was – and never will be – a single Arab opinion, and not least during the Second World War. Relatively few Arabs joined the half-hearted local clones of the European fascist parties. Despite their antipathy to colonialism, perhaps a majority of Arab leaders tended to sympathise with the Allies. Despite the size of the pro-Vichy forces, the number of Arabs who volunteered for the fight alongside the Axis was small compared with those who enlisted with the British and Free French. The extreme anti-Jewish sentiments such as those espoused by the Grand Mufti were contrasted by many Arab families who sheltered Jews during the Axis occupation of Tunisia. In Morocco, for example, King Mohammed V refused to make the 200,000 Moroccan Jews wear yellow stars (although this awful discrimination was practised in France).

Islamism was manipulated by all sides in the propaganda campaigns of the 1939-45 war. Most of it was mere window dressing. Where it was believed, passionately, was a movement formed in 1928 – the Muslim Brotherhood. The immediate years of the Cold War, however, witnessed an age of dictators and Arab nationalism marked by secularism not Islamism. The Egyptian man on horseback, Gamal Abdel Nasser, the most charismatic of Arab leaders, dealt a fatal blow to British power during the Suez crisis of 1956. He also assisted Arab nationalists to defeat the French in Algeria. The new Arab dictators were each courted by the rival superpowers in Moscow and Washington. The US protected the oil and ruling family in Saudi Arabia, while Washington also backed the Shia leadership under the shah in Iran. Many of the Arab leaders forgot their socialist mantras and became corrupt oligarchies, buttressed by their security forces. The *Mukhabarat*, the secret service, was often the most, and sometimes only, efficient state organ. Washington rarely protested on the simple principle: 'He may be a bastard, but he's our bastard.' Meanwhile, the Arab-Israeli confrontation festered. This was often portrayed as the central problem of Arab politics. On the contrary, it was the only thing the Arab League could usually agree on. The Arab world would have been far more fractious without the existence of a common enemy, Zionism.

From Cold War to War on Terror

Western and Islamic scholars disagree as to when and why the jihad intensified and the clamour to revive the caliphate was sparked. Some Muslim historians focus on the sins of Israel, notably winning the 'war of independence in 1948-9'. Arabs and particularly the Palestinians refer to this as the *Nakba* – the day of catastrophe. They also point to the utter humiliation of the Six-Day War in 1967. The constant failure of Arab armies required a scapegoat – especially American military support whipped up by Jewish lobbies. The humiliation of Egyptian armies in Yemen added to the collapse of belief in secular Arab socialism as the way forward. Perhaps God should be given a chance, or so a growing minority began to think.

An Islamic revolution deposed the American-backed shah in Iran. In the same year the Soviets invaded Afghanistan – that would lead to the influx of holy warriors, *Mujahedin,* from the entire Muslim world. The exodus of Russian troops in 1989 was celebrated by Islamists everywhere as a vindication of Allah's blessings. Islamic warriors had defeated a superpower – now for the American Satan. Most contemporary combat-experienced *Mujahedin* will insist that Bosnia played a big part in the revival of jihadism. In the small and newest country in Europe, foreign *Mujahedin* rushed in to protect the vulnerable Muslim communities on the frontier of the *Umma.* It was where, as P.J. O'Rourke famously quipped, 'the unpronounceables were killing the unspellables'. Thereafter foreign volunteers, especially the tough Chechens, were fired up to fight not just the Russians but throughout the jihadist international. The wars against Saddam Hussein and the alleged presence of unclean uniformed American soldiers, especially women, near the holy places in Saudi Arabia were also volatile accelerants. Meanwhile, Islamist insurgency spread in Asia, in the Philippines and in Indonesia. In Africa the implosion of Somalia left the ungoverned spaces ripe for jihadists to exploit.

The al-Qaeda strategic masterstroke, the 9/11 attacks on the heart of the Americans, was considered a major counter-blow to the Western crusade in the Middle East. Many Arab states, however, were privately prepared to accept the American reprisal in toppling the Taliban in 2001. The removal of Saddam Hussein in 2003, if not condoned by all members of the Arab League, was quietly tolerated because Saddam was not a popular figure, especially after his invasion of Kuwait. In fact, he was loathed by nearly all other Arab leaders. The occupation fiasco in Iraq immediately raised hackles, however. Paul Bremer was the US State Department official who was in charge of the immediate occupation period. He ran his own show, very badly. Former Speaker of the House Newt Gingrich called him 'the single largest disaster in American foreign policy in modern times'. The jihadist response abroad came soon. Atrocities in Europe, for example the bombings on the London transport system in 2005, were seen by jihadists as the inevitable consequences of Western attacks on the *Umma*. This was dramatised by Hamas's defence against the Israelis and the perceived double standards of the West towards the Jewish state.

The Arab Spring of 2011 was welcomed in the West as a means of undermining the radical message of al-Qaeda and its expanding franchises blossoming in North Africa and Yemen. Western chancelleries hoped that the indigenous toppling of tyrants, even if pro-Western, would finally introduce a new dawn of liberal democracies. Remember that the fall of Saddam was supposed to be the key to unlock democracy in the Middle East and to contradict those cynics who believed that Arabs were not fit or ready for democracy; that Islam preferred men on horseback.

As Robert Fisk, the well-known British writer on the region, put it so aptly: 'We like dictatorships. We know how to do business with the kings and generals – how to sell them our tanks and fighter-bombers and missiles.' Instead, with Libya being the prime example, dictatorships gave way to mayhem. The political vacuum created by the fall of Colonel Gaddafi was filled not by Jeffersonian democrats but by bloodthirsty Islamist extremists. In Libya NATO had inadvertently acted as the air wing of al-Qaeda, soon to be displaced by the more dangerous Islamic State. Libya was awash with weapons that were dispersed to fanatics in Algeria, Mali, Nigeria and elsewhere in the arid Sahara and Sahel. Soon, from A-Z – Algeria to Zanzibar – jihadist groups, most egregiously Boko Haram in Nigeria, rushed to swear allegiance to the new caliphate.

It is amazing that the Sykes-Picot dispensation lasted so long – nearly a century. Most of the artificial states and borders conjured up by the British and French bureaucrats made little sense in 1916, let alone today. The whole edifice of the Middle East was collapsing, so it was not surprising that a new wave of jihadism should reject not just the cartographic lunacy of a century ago but also the whole Arab political firmament – indeed anything not specifically ordained by Allah.

The emergence of the Islamic State

Three major Western interventions helped to regenerate the Islamic State crisis of 2014-17: Afghanistan, Iraq and Libya – all states whose borders were designed by imperial fiat. Western diplomacy stumbled elsewhere but the bloody anarchy in these three countries was paramount. That is not to say that Western military action in these three states was solely responsible, the only recruiting sergeants for the jihadist cause – just as Israel is not the sole factor, despite its use as a whipping boy for all Arab woes. Or just as African states still resort to blaming colonialism for their calamities instead of examining their own arrogant and incompetent governance. The American-led interventions in Afghanistan and Iraq and the more reluctant involvement in Libya did create, however, numerous unintended consequences. For example, the destruction of the Ba'athist regime in Baghdad was directly responsible for the unchecked rise of Iran, one of Washington's great *bêtes noires*. Even worse, the growth of jihadist forces in Afghanistan, Iraq and Libya caused murderous 'blowbacks' in the West, not least the training of young jihadists keen to bomb the Western heartlands in retaliation for what they perceived as Western atrocities in the *Umma*.

Other Muslim countries were also involved with the rise of the Islamic State. Pakistanis or Pakistani territory were previously involved in 75 per cent of jihadist attacks in the UK, although the focus has recently shifted to IS. The billions spent by NATO on fighting the Taliban in Afghanistan could have been better spent on neutering the Pakistani threat, not least from its loose nukes. Our so-called ally in Afghanistan – namely Pakistan – was our main enemy. Regarding the nukes, the Saudis – the other great enemy of the West – have been paying for Pakistan's nukes. Riyadh may well cash in its chips if it perceives that the Shi'ite challenge from nuclear Iran is getting too hot. If Pakistan has batted on both sides, so has Saudi Arabia. It was the epicentre of the Wahhabi creed espoused by al-Qaeda and later IS. Riyadh – via its 'Riyalpolitik' – officially or through individual Saudi billionaires has sent money to a bewildering array of Islamist groups nominally to pay for charitable causes or new madrassahs but often to fund terrorist training and weapons throughout the Middle East and Asia.

With allies like these how could the West hope to win its battles with its declared jihadist enemies? The strategic intention of 9/11 was to provoke Western forces to overreact, invade and radicalise Muslims worldwide. Thus Osama bin Laden achieved what he set out to do although he did not live long enough to see the caliphate established. Jihadism is a far more dangerous foe to the West now than in 9/11 or 7/7.

For a while it looked as though the Arab Spring would lead to the same liberalisation as in Eastern Europe. Nearly all the Western foreign correspondents were wrong about believing, and predicting, this – just as they failed to foretell the rapid fall of the Soviet empire. The removal of Saddam was supposed to be the key to unlock democracy in the region. Then one single flutter of a butterfly's wings set off a massive regional storm. It was an economic not a political act. At 11.30 am on 17 December 2010, in the small town of Sidi Bouzid in rural Tunisia, a vegetable seller named Mohamed Bouazizi immolated himself with a can of petrol outside the governor's office. It was the ultimate protest against corruption and the harassment of small businesses. North African countries were all unhappy in their own distinctive ways but most of the grievances were not political but economic – mainly lack of employment for young people. Although the Tunisian vegetable seller's desperation was fired up by economic anger soon his revolt became political – governments fell throughout the region. Initially the West did not know how to react yet hoped that local democracy could undercut the jihadist appeal of al-Qaeda, as well as introduce long-needed reform, even if it meant backing off from friendly dictators in countries such as Egypt. Initially, Barack Obama compared the Arab revolts to the US rejection of British colonialism. 'Our people fought a painful Civil War that extended freedom and dignity to those who were enslaved,' the President added. Washington had a problem: the Egyptian military dictatorship was a stalwart ally so how could the popular rebellions against it be publicly encouraged? The worst result for the West was in Libya. Chaos, a tsunami of migrants and weapons, plus the rapid advance of jihadism, not just in Libya, but throughout the Sahel, was not what NATO had signed up for. The Russians and Chinese also felt cheated – they signed up at the UN for humanitarian action, not full-scale military intervention to achieve regime change. The Libyan debacle exacerbated extensive existing Russian and Chinese suspicions of Western intentions. Once more, Western military intervention had created an avalanche of unintended consequences.

The West was damned for the aftermath of its interventionism in Afghanistan, Iraq and Libya. Then the West was damned for *not* intervening directly in the first years of the Syrian civil war. With this partial exception in Syria, al-Qaeda had largely been contained in the Middle East if not North Africa. Meanwhile in the war of ideas and social media, the West had been completely outgunned. Soon the warriors of the caliphate would become masters of the universe compared with the plodding propagandists in London and Washington. The Islamists created highly emotive videos on YouTube that could seduce young and old throughout the *Umma*. They deftly deployed social media to reach into the bedrooms of disaffected young Muslims to groom them into believing the paradise of the caliphate awaited them. The jihadist war was ratcheted up to a much more rapid tempo in Europe and the Middle East. The 'pure' caliphate had been reborn – it had been the dream of Islamists for generations, if not centuries.

On 29 June 2014 the new worldwide caliphate was declared, claiming the allegiance of Muslims everywhere: 1.6 billion people, a quarter of the planet's population. In effect, war was also declared on the remaining members of the planet who were *not* practising Sunni Muslims. The caliphate was led by Abu Bakr al-Baghdadi, a *nom de guerre,* who announced the new state in a sermon in Mosul's main al-Nuri mosque. This was novel – al-Qaeda had *talked* of a caliphate one fine day but now a territorial Islamist entity had been created. It was said to be the most pious strand of Salafist Sunni militant jihadism. All Muslims were urged to join the only state that was true to the original ideals of the Prophet. Like his seventh-century inspiration, the new state was based on amazing military gains in Iraq and Syria.

The multiple crises in Europe today in some respects mirror the chaos in the international system that permitted the rapid advance of the Muslim armies in the seventh and eighth centuries. One of the biggest dangers is mass migration, partly caused by Western interventions, Assad's atrocities and the jihadist-induced carnage in Arab lands. It is deeply ironic that the new caliphate is calling for Muslims to heed the trumpet-call to join the Islamic utopia, when millions and millions of Muslims are fleeing IS depredations and the general mayhem that passes for political life in the region. An interesting parallel exists. Zionists used to tell Western Jews to give up their decadent materialism for the breezy austerity of pioneer life in Israel, while at the same time encouraging local Arabs to give up their nationalism in exchange for the economic advantages of trading with and working for the Israeli *Wirtschaftswunder*. *Aliya* to Israel has generally worked for most Jews, although the *hegirah* to the Islamic State has generally proved fatal for Muslims.

It was one of the paradoxes of the Arab Spring that Syria's president, Bashar al-Assad, became demonised – just like Saddam and Gaddafi – and yet he later became a crucial if implicit ally of the West in the war on Islamic State, after helping it initially, just as Turkey did. The West completely underestimated Assad and the determination of Iran and then Russia to keep him in power. The endgame in Syria is unclear, although it looks as if the territorial shelf-life of the Islamic State is about to expire. It will morph into something else somewhere else. The fight against IS, at the time of writing, is in full spate in both Syria and Iraq. How was this war fought internationally and domestically in the West? And with what likely results?

Chapter 5

Taking on the Islamists

The International Front

Tony Blair's ten years in power left the British military in tatters. The Labour leader asked his military to police the world – and it largely accepted without much kickback – and then the prime minister refused to pay the bill. Thus the British forces lost two wars, British military standing in Washington and its own confidence. The Americans too lost both wars. In 2017 they are back training and fighting in Iraq and are now sending more forces to Syria and Afghanistan.

David Cameron came to power promising a more humble foreign policy. He said, 'You cannot drop a fully formed democracy out of an aeroplane at 40,000 feet.' And yet the new limited foreign policy conjured up pandemonium in Libya. President Obama also wanted a more restrained and patient foreign policy. He promised to end the engagement in Iraq; he did so, perhaps precipitously, and then ordered a severe drawdown in Afghanistan. The Taliban – plus some IS remnants – look like taking over that sad country. Obama's biggest humiliation was in Syria. Palmyra was only of symbolic and historical significance to Assad; Aleppo was his prize. The world watched in horror as the Damascus government starved and bombed its population (or its Islamist captors) into surrender. Assad won there – and possibly in the whole civil war – because of Russian bombers and special forces, Iranian Revolutionary Guards, Hezbollah militias – and American indifference (until Trump stepped in). Others would blame Obama's invertebracy – yet the first black president had shown courage in giving the go-ahead to take out Osama bin Laden hiding almost in plain sight in Pakistan. This could have easily been a replay of Jimmy Carter's failed intervention in Iran to rescue the American hostages. In 2013 Obama did not honour his own 'red line', allowing Assad to escape accountability for the (disputed) chemical attack in his own capital. Obama could not win this one – if he had intervened he would have been blamed just as much as for his non-intervention. But history will judge if this refusal was his 'Rwanda moment'. Obama also made himself a prisoner of his own legacy in the nuclear accord with Iran. Flush with cash released by the deal, Iranian hardliners felt they could get away with murder – literally. They embarked on an aggressive Shi'ite adventurism not seen in a century or two. Iran did not need nuclear weapons to conquer Aleppo and to dominate Syrian, Iraqi, Lebanese and Yemeni politics. The old enemy Sunni Saudi Arabia and their American friends were all sidelined by the Shia resurgence.

The Arab Spring became a deep winter of discontent. The great tragedy was that it lacked a narrative. It was not a drive for democracy but just a desperate rejection of the status quo, initially the lack of business opportunities for young people swamped by ubiquitous corruption. Arab states have declined dramatically – some no longer exist as the unitary states they pretended to be – Syria, Iraq, Yemen and Libya. Except for the oil-rich and population-poor Gulf states, most have failed to match population growth with economic advance. The Arab world was 280 million in 2000 and perhaps 380 million now – no wonder so many Arabs have wanted to chase jobs in Europe. Maybe we should not talk about the Arab Middle East any more. They remain the largest ethnic group but they are politically and economically hobbled. The former Arab power players such as Egypt, Syria and Iraq are but ghosts of their former selves. The Saudis, some would argue, are an exception. The oil price has humbled them too, and their involvement in Syria has produced nothing, while their bombing campaigns in Yemen have alienated even their friends. Above all, the Saudis have completely failed to curb the Iranian advance.

The void of Arab power has been filled by non-Arab states such as Iran and Turkey – and, to a far lesser degree, Israel. Both Iran and Turkey are not recent artificial colonial creations like many of the Arab states. Their venerable cultures have created more sustainable and cohesive pseudo-modern states. Arab nationalism – epitomised by Nasser – promised so much, and yet at the time of writing it is exactly half a century since that dream was shattered by the Israeli victory in the Six-Day War. Arab secular nationalism's humiliation was of course a spur to Islamism. Arab nationalism did in theory aim to unite all Arabs; Islamism, however, has accelerated the division of the Arab world, not least the Shia and Sunni schism. Such sectarianism has also undermined internal alliances not least with persecuted minorities such as the Christians. They were often the commercial cement in many Arab states; just like Jewish businessmen before them, these ancient Christian communities have been driven out, most savagely in Iraq. Their position is threatened throughout the Arab world, even in the traditionally more tolerant Egypt.

Compared with the USSR, Putin's Russia is a pocket superpower. Nevertheless, Russian military power has also filled a void left by the American recessional in the region. This is back to the future when the USSR leapfrogged over NATO's northern tier to engage with Nasser at the height of the Cold War. Russian arms could not prevent the humiliation of the 1967 war with Israel and so Egypt and Jordan withdrew from the order of battle lined up against the Jewish state. The Arab-Israeli conflict declined as the core of regional disputes. That does not mean that an Israeli-Palestinian deal – a real one – would not do much to reduce tensions in a devastated region.

Obama bombed seven countries during his reign – although his preferred mode of operation was the deployment of armed drones. His redline cock-up in Syria was perhaps a little like Dean Acheson's failure to include Korea in his famous Perimeter Speech. Whether that caused the Korean War or not, it does indicate the danger of drawing lines – especially if you don't act to protect them. It allows regional bullies to push to the limits; and then beyond them. Arguably, the same happened with Saddam's invasion of Kuwait. After his capture he said, 'Do you think I would really have brought the full weight of American power down on my head if I had realised they would react like that to the Iraqi liberation of Kuwait?'

The IS endgame

The declaration of the caliphate in 2014 shook the region's foundations perhaps as much as Israel's emergence in 1948. In 2016 Trump's surprise victory threatened to completely transform US foreign policy. He said in his election campaign that he had a 'Secret Foolproof Plan' to remove the Islamic State from the face of the earth. This was, however, 'fake news'. No plan existed, although the outgoing Democratic president did have a short plan with various options. One was to (better) arm the Syrian Kurds, allies of the PKK, designated terrorists by Turkey as well as by the US. Another was to continue to arm former al-Qaeda-aligned groups (which incidentally breaks US law). On the campaign trail the unsubtle Trump said, 'I would bomb the shit out of them.' The coalition air operations so far had been dubbed 'anaemic' by most insiders. And yet a replay of a comprehensive blitzkrieg along the lines of Operation DESERT STORM, which liberated Kuwait in 1991, is not on the cards. Already, US-led air attacks against the Islamic State are probably killing more civilians in the two states than the Russians did (proportionately) in Aleppo.

Western media played up the siege of Aleppo where the Syrian army was trying to break the grip of al-Qaeda-aligned fighters. The media created a moral panic about siege warfare and trapped civilians. And yet the liberation of Mosul had been soft-soaped despite American-led aerial bombing and starvation as bad if not worse than Aleppo. The fighting in Mosul in 2017 has been the most bitter and extensive urban warfare since 1945 (including the Chechen capital, Grozny). It was right to free both cities from Islamist control but the different propaganda perspectives were striking. Tear away the propaganda veils and it was apparent that the sieges in both Aleppo and Mosul were very similar. In both cases forces loyal to an internationally recognised government were attacking heavily populated cities with the aid of foreign air power. Both cities were under the dominance of armed Islamist fighters who were holding much of the civilian population hostage.

One overwhelming question remains: how did IS last so long, especially as eventually the whole world was aligned against it? The vastly

(right) The Moroccan ambassador to London, sent to persuade Queen Elizabeth I to form an Anglo-Moroccan front against Spain and the Caliphate in Istanbul.

(below) Gertrude Bell should be more famous than Lawrence of Arabia for forging the shape of the Middle East.

(*Left*) Memorial in Washington D.C. to commemorate the US dead in the Korea War. Could Americans soon be fighting on the peninsula again? (*Author*)

(*Below*) The former KGB HQ in Lukiškės Square in Vilnius, the Lithuanian capital. Thousands of Lithuanians were shot inside its thick walls.

After walking out of Afghanistan, *Mujahedin* relax in the tribal area between Afghanistan and Pakistan. The group had seen a lot of combat during a major Soviet offensive, June 1984. Author is in the centre with a Coke. (*Author's collection*)

Ukrainian military museum, near Kiev, shows how intertwined Russian and Ukrainian defence production has been – especially in helicopter design. (*Author*)

Palestinian woman sits stoically outside her ruined house during the siege of Jenin, in the West Bank, in May 2002. Her house had been sliced through by a massive Israeli armoured bulldozer. (*Author*)

The fall of the Berlin Wall did not bring an 'end of history'.

The first Chechen war (1994–96).

British troops on patrol near Umm Qasr in the first weeks of the occupation of southern Ira.
(*Author*)

The Americans used cruise missiles to destroy the Al-Shifa medical factory in Khartou.
in August 1998. Washington alleged it was a chemical weapons factory. It was an innoce:
facility for producing anti-malaria drugs. (*Author*)

ATO forces patrolling over Afghanistan. (*NATO*)

lamic State liked to compare their initial advance with the military victories of the
rst caliphate.

(*Left*) German armoured vehicle in Kabul with NATO forces in 2002. Strange to see the German cross on armour and active in foreign lands again. (*Author*)

(*Below*) Islamic State forces celebrating early victories in Raqqa, their capital.

The new caliphate was declared on 29 June 2014 by the caliph, Abu-Bakr al-Baghdadi.

GCHQ in Cheltenham, England, is the centre of British cyber warfare and defence.

(*Above*) Islamists often criticised Muslim participation in UK elections because they were considered hostile to Sharia law.

(*Left*) Front cover of *Dabiq*, the glossy propaganda magazine produced by IS.

Anti-Gaddafi graffito in Tripoli in the uprising during the Arab Spring. (*NATO*)

The Eurofighter Typhoon was deployed in combat in Libya and is now operational in the Baltic states.

B-2 Spirit stealth bomber. (*DoD*)

HMS *Queen Elizabeth*, the new Royal Navy carrier, but with no planes to adorn its deck, ye

im Jong-un: 'Is that the US Navy out there?'

hina's first aircraft carrier, the *Liaoning*.

Massoud Barzani, the president of Iraqi Kurdistan.

Michel Houellebecq, controversial French author of *Submission*.

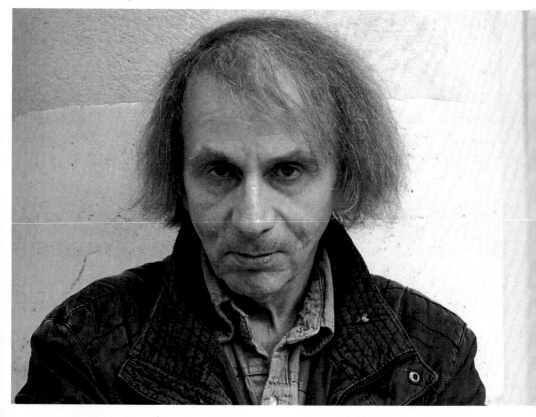

esident Trump has relied on a number of generals, especially H.R. McMaster, his National curity Adviser.

he bogus photo-shopped picture that went viral on the Internet. It parodied the alleged over-endliness between Trump and Putin – before the US president's cruise missile attack on Syria.

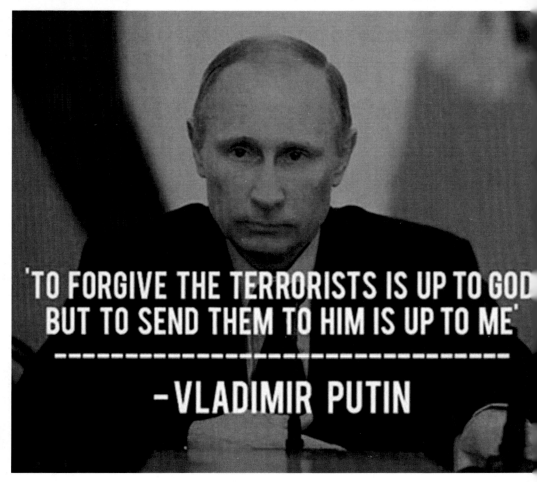

Viral hit.

Concept of new Russian Armata T-14.

superior firepower of the massive coalition of Western and Muslim states did not concentrate its strength to wipe out the capital in Raqqa, for example. Why? Never before in history had a landlocked state, without any naval or air assets, resisted nearly all the great powers. It is not difficult to understand why pious Muslims would see the hand of God in all this.

Conspiracy theories abound, with the most startling – that Caliph al-Baghdadi was an Israeli plant and Jewish to boot – rather beyond the pale. That Assad and Washington helped to create IS is less so. Let's look at the provable facts, however. One part of the answer is that for many of the protagonists crushing the Islamist state was not a top priority. Other long-standing interests held sway. Take Turkey. Ankara was always more concerned with getting rid of Assad and containing Kurdish autonomy. The Saudis were obsessed with deterring Shia Iran rather than fellow Sunni Wahhabis running the Islamic State, which was anyway chock-full of Saudi fighters and imams – and money initially. Russia was concerned with using Syria to restore its regional influence and, although Putin hated Islamists, he spent little time attacking IS. In short, IS was not the prime enemy of many of the participants. This dynamic extended the war and augmented the chaos.

And America, which headed the international anti-IS coalition? Obama was determined *not* to enter another Middle East war – he had won the White House partly on the promise of ending foreign entanglements especially in the Islamic world. If that was the strategic impediment – all the tactical elements were wrong as well. Obama (and London) insisted that Assad had to go before a settlement could be reached. Washington refused to engage with Moscow on an anti-IS campaign. They talked mainly (though not only) about de-conflicting their air wars, not least after US-led aircraft hit Syrian government forces fighting IS troops, killing possibly as many as eighty elite troops. America also pretended that Turkey was a steadfast ally when on the ground, especially with US support for Syrian Kurdish militias, Washington ended up, in effect, fighting against Turkish troops. The US State Department (if not the Pentagon) also hung on foolishly to the theory that there really were significant numbers of non-Islamist 'moderate' Syrian opposition forces.

Trump, however, wanted go for a quick win against IS if he could; that would mean more and heavier air attacks, more US special forces, and more guns for the Kurds. *Who* appears to win in Raqqa and Mosul, both currently under close siege, will matter. The Shia-dominated Baghdad government, for example, tried to keep its Shi'ite militias under wraps. Arab Sunnis, not Kurds, will be presented as liberators of Raqqa. The Sunni sense of grievance in both countries is virulent.

By early 2017 it looked as though Assad was doing well. Trump had made it clear that he wanted to leave Assad in place and concentrate on IS. Regime change was firmly off the American agenda. Then two things went wrong for the Syrian president: Assad overreached and Trump changed his mind. The gas attacks on eighty-plus civilians triggered fifty-nine cruise missiles on the Syrian-Russian air base where the gas attacks allegedly originated. Whatever the final provenance of the weapons turns out to be, Assad and his generals took Trump at his word. A big mistake. They never thought the new isolationist president would act, no matter what outrage was conjured up by Damascus.

If the chief strategists in Raqqa were prone to such things, then the corks would have been popping after Trump took the pressure off them. For a while. Nevertheless, the Islamic State will shrink and be completely overrun but it will not 'fall'. IS borders will give way to less tangible fronts. The idea of a caliphate – established by the Prophet himself – is too powerful to die. The Islamic State has been a cruel mutation of the Islamist dream but it may metamorphose into a looser organisation akin to its predecessor, al-Qaeda. Yet one of the dominant differences with the rival Islamist grouping has been its claim to territorial power. The propagandists in IS are already talking about re-forming elsewhere – including a new 'army of conquest' in America. A virtual caliphate will persist, and the physical manifestation may re-emerge perhaps in the 'provinces' that have already sworn allegiance such as Sinai, the Sahel, eastern Libya and elsewhere in the Maghreb. Vulcan's Mr Spock would deploy his logic to say that the obvious new home is in Saudi Arabia, in its original location between Mecca and Medina. If the Saudi royals' house of cards collapses then a radical form of Wahhabi republic will no doubt materialise.

The end of the current Islamic State should weaken the Islamist project. After all, Caliph Abu Bakr al-Baghdadi said in his inaugural Mosul sermon that he was doing the work of Allah. Either Allah got it wrong or his interpreters did. The End Timers will have to wait a bit longer. As with nearly all such eschatological prophecies that inevitably miss their date with destiny, cognitive dissonance sets in. Facts are re-interpreted to fit the predominant beliefs – rather like the Trump White House. Having said that, according to the Book of Revelation, Armageddon is the prophesied location of the battle that will precipitate the End Times. The plains of Armageddon are disturbingly close to where the Syrian civil war is being fought out. Armed clashes between the world's superpowers in the end-game in Syria should perhaps be avoided.

After IS collapse the acts of foreign jihadist terrorism will mount probably, not least with so many bitter and hardcore European fighters returning home from the ashes of their dreams. Hundreds if not thousands of jihadists have been told to smuggle themselves back into Europe for future 'operations'. A dirty bomb is still an alluring terrorist ambition. Radioactive contamination in the City of London may kill relatively few people but it could mean a very lengthy decontamination that could strike a dagger at the heart of the post-Brexit British economy. This would be a weapon of mass effect rather than mass destruction.

Since Jesus Christ was crucified Christianity has changed with the times (outside some American southern states). Islam has altered very little since the Prophet departed from this earth. Unless Islam reforms itself and finds its own enlightenment (again) – only Muslims themselves can achieve this – the religion will be left to stagnate even more in terms of scientific development and governance. Islamic governments are nearly everywhere chaotic and/or murderous. Turkey and Tunisia were once beacons of Islamic hope. Ankara is now mired in bloodshed and authoritarianism, especially since the tarnished victory in the April 2017 referendum allowed President Erdogan to become an embryonic caliph. Tunisia is a world leader in producing jihadists and its tourist economy has been crushed by terrorism; as an Islamist bonus the beaches have far less booze, bikinis and unbelievers. With this kind of Islamic context, no wonder the Islamic State flourished – for a while

The home front

In a world of globalised commerce and media, globalised terrorism should not be surprising. Muslims have been radicalised by IS and by highly publicised dramas such as Israel's retaliations against Hamas in Gaza. Thousands of Western-born Muslims have been sucked into the holy war waged by IS. Some have been killed but more will return to Europe after escaping the sieges of Raqqa and Mosul. Some come back chastened and disillusioned, keen on regular showers and a place to charge, and use, their smartphones. A dangerous and committed minority has returned to wage jihad at home. Probably about 15 per cent of returnees remain active jihadists who admit to counter-terrorism officers that they want to continue the fight in the UK. Of course many returnees remain shtum. Short of locking up *all* returnees, it is sometimes hard to decide whether those who bonded together in Syria will not bomb together in England.

Operating a comprehensive census was not an IS priority so figures will be vague. Perhaps up to 5,000 Muslims from Europe travelled to IS after the call to arms in 2014. Probably over 850 Brits went and, at time of writing, maybe 400 remain, dead or alive, in the shrinking enclaves. Were IS a real state, then each citizen who travelled to fight could be guilty of treason, let alone any war crimes they may have committed. Despite the liberalisation of the British penal code, beheading innocent civilians is still a punishable offence, provided the Crown Prosecution Service can prove it. The CPS likes lots of files, and surprisingly the IS bureaucrats have paid more than a touch of Nazi-style attention to written records. British citizens who have been IS operatives have been summarily wiped out by coalition air strikes, whether or not they were armed and whether or not it could be proved (publicly) they posed an imminent threat to the UK.

They are treated as combatants. Here is the inconsistency. When Britain confronts IS in Syria and Iraq the armed forces behave as if they are at war with a foreign power. And yet if an IS fighter makes it back to the UK he or she is treated as a civilian with all the rights of citizenship, including expensive legal aid at the taxpayers' expense. Despite all the terror legislation that has been enacted in the last decade or so, treason has not been properly redefined. If a Brit willingly travels to join IS (or its successor) he or she should be prosecuted under a new treason law (way beyond the former proverbial 'arson in the Queen's dockyard'). Travelling to ally oneself with the likes of a deadly and barbaric Islamist state should result in a long prison sentence – not the more customary slap on the wrist.

Terrorism convictions have doubled in the UK since 2012 – some of them related to right-wing actions. The government likes to point out that up to 25 per cent of those 'treated' under the anti-radicalisation Prevent strategy are white British right-wingers. And yet the type of despicable person who killed Labour MP Jo Cox is home grown and usually stay-at-home. So the issue of foreign-born Islamists, some with dual citizenship, does not apply. Increased efforts have been made to exclude British citizens from returning to the UK, however. Powers to strip dual nationals of their British citizenship have been used at least thirty-three times on terrorism-related grounds since 2010. They were ruled legal in March 2017 by the European Court of Human Rights. One high-profile example is Asma al-Assad, the glamorous British-born wife of the Syrian president. She used to adorn *Vogue* profiles as a 'rose in the desert'. Syria's first lady has been a very active propagandist on social media including defending her husband against accusations of gassing children. Born in Acton, West London, she holds both British and Syrian nationality so removing her British nationality is unlikely to be considered illegal. Ministers can remove the citizenship of Brits with single-nationality if they were previously citizens of another country and can 'temporarily exclude' British-born citizens from returning to Britain. The hook-handed hate preacher Abu Hamza's son, Sufiyan Mustafa, 22, was stopped from returning to |Britain after fighting in Syria. But these powers are rarely deployed.

There is no power to permanently remove the citizenship of someone who was born British. A person cannot be made stateless. But if EU anti-Brexit propaganda is to be believed British citizens could be allowed to keep EU citizenship if they opted for it. This could be a legal and cost-effective way of MI5 getting rid of a large number of troublesome UK jihadists.

Excluding dangerous Islamists is just one small part of the story. The key question is integration. Multiculturalism has clearly failed – all it has produced is dangerous ghettoes. In some wards in the Midland cities the concentration of Muslims is so intense that some of the children living there responded to a school survey by guessing that the UK was up to 75 per cent Muslim. Most Islamist terrorists come from London but others are concentrated in, for example, Birmingham; twenty-six of Birmingham's thirty-nine terrorist offenders came from just six small wards around Hodge Hill, where Labour MP and former minister Liam Byrne has focused his anti-Islamist campaigns.[1] He was also infamous as the outgoing former chief of the Treasury under Gordon Brown who left a note for the incoming Lib-Dem-Tory coalition saying 'There is no money left.'

It is odd that, at the same time as apartheid in South Africa was the cause *du jour* in the UK, social apartheid was encouraged in many poorer Asian suburbs. Pakistanis and Bangladeshis have lived parallel but separate lives. The lack of integration and the resulting ghettoes spawned nurseries of radicalisation. Trojan horse schools still flourish where state schools are infiltrated by Islamist entryists. Or illegal private religious schools have sprouted, where Ofsted does not enter. In fifteen months during 2015-2016 British school inspectors came across 241 suspected illegal schools in England, far more than was estimated. Voting rackets have created rotten pocket boroughs, most famously in the so-called Islamic Republic of Tower Hamlets. The stereotype of some terrorists as isolated lone wolves is not usually accurate. More than three-quarters were part of strong families and communities. The families and mosques often deny any knowledge of radicalisation to the police. Well, they would, wouldn't they? – to misquote Mandy Rice-Davies. While it is also true that a small minority of terrorists are pariahs in their own communities, many are not. The problem is very few Muslims will report their suspicions to the Prevent teams because the various (often squabbling) Muslim associations have characterised the government's counter-terrorism strategy as a form of Islamophobic spying. Baroness Warsi, the former Tory minister for faith and communities from 2012 to 2014, said that the Prevent strategy was 'broken' and should be 'paused'.

The police and other authorities were often kept away from cases of domestic violence, forced marriage, and genital mutilation; not all were Muslim perpetrators but the closed nature of Islamic society added to the wall of silence. When young girls were taken from school and sent to Pakistan – to find frequently much older husbands – often the violation was not investigated. The need to sustain political correctness induced some police forces to ignore many crimes, not least the Pakistani sex-grooming gangs in thirty cities but most notoriously in Rotherham. Also, medical authorities have been reluctant to speak out against marriage with cousins. The practice was long prohibited in the Judeo-Christian tradition but was sanctioned by the Prophet. In England more than half of Pakistani immigrants are married to their cousins. Again, Muslims are not the only ones involved. Such genetic inbreeding had caused famous deformities in Christian European royal families. Royal births are statistically rare, though. Pakistanis are responsible, however, for 3 per cent of births in the UK, yet they account for 33 per cent of children with birth defects. Some of the defects last for life and cause massive costs to the health and educational systems. It would be kind, and practical, to ban consanguineous marriages. It would save the NHS a small fortune and increase the IQs of the relevant community by 10-16 per cent. Such a law might be too late to help the intellectual standards of the House of Windsor, though.

The collapse of the Islamic State will presumably mean an end to the migration from the West to Syria, which is already a small trickle because IS had lost control of the border with Turkey. The would-be jihadi brides will have to fixate on something else. Leaving home and rebelling against their parents was a delicious teenage combination. Some of the young men will continue to feel a sense of oppression and self-justified rage that inspires many young Muslims who feel alienated from the job market in particular and British culture in general. MI5 refers to this as 'blocked mobility'. Polls suggest that half of British Muslims admit to wanting Sharia in Britain and many use Sharia courts for non-criminal issues, even if they don't formally advocate the ISIB – the Islamic State of Ireland and Britain.

Many of these issues I discussed in detail in my *Jihadist Threat* book and they still apply. Muslims complain of Islamophobia increasingly but the intelligence services and police complain equally about the lack of co-operation from Muslims. Muslims are a broad church, if they will forgive the phrase. In a sense this is not a single clash of civilisations; it is about a massive array of Muslims from different sects, countries and cultures, many of whom disagree with the corruption of Islam which IS represents. The Islamist State is a result of a clash *within* the Islamic civilisation caused by a smallish cult which has a large following, much of it passive, throughout the Muslim world. Not enough of the nearly 3 million British Muslims (half of whom are under 25) condemn Islamism in general or particular examples they may come across. According to a recent ICM poll, two thirds of British Muslims would refuse to 'grass up' a fellow Muslim 'no matter how much ricin he was storing in their lock-ups', to quote controversial *Sunday Times* columnist Rod Liddle. Very few want to integrate and most profess views on Jewish people 'which Ernst Röhm would have thought a bit gamey' – to quote Liddle again. More British Muslims believe that 'the Jews' were behind 9/11 than think it was al-Qaeda. Walk around any bazaar or shopping centre in the Middle East, however, and the Mossad/CIA conspiracy would rate as around 90 per cent responsible.

Iran's supreme leader Grand Ayatollah Ali Khameini once urged Muslims to boycott anything and everything that originated with the Jewish people. So any devout Muslim who has syphilis should not be cured by Salvarsan-type medicines first discovered by a Jewish scientist, Dr Paul Ehrlich. And so on. Fundamentalist Muslims should suffer syphilis, gonorrhoea, heart disease, headaches, typhus, diabetes, mental disorders, polio convulsions and TB and thus be proud to obey the Islamic boycott. If the pious Muslim patient is still alive he should not ring his or her doctor on a cell phone, originally invented in Israel by a Jewish engineer. Muslims, despite their large numbers, have contributed to very few Nobel prizes, especially compared with the overwhelming number of Jewish recipients. It has to do partly with open-mindedness and good education – as well as not marrying your cousin.

Arabs tend to blame the overall Jewish conspiracy for many of their ills, especially since the specific CIA-Mossad conspiracy to topple the Twin Towers. In the UK Muslims tend to blame everyone else for perceived Islamophobia, Moslems should invest more in education, especially scientific education, and less on theology. And they should start condemning Islamist violence far more often and not proclaim that Islam is a religion of peace. As the saying goes, 'If the Arabs put down their weapons today, there would be no more violence. If the Jews put down their weapons today, there would be no more Israel.' And British Muslims might not approve of throwing gays off tall buildings IS-style but tolerance towards gays hardly exists at all. I don't know what radical British Islamists make of Jewish gays.

Reform

The violence associated with IS has everything to do with Islam, the worst kind of Islam, yes, but Islam nonetheless. No religion is entirely peaceful but Islam is specifically not. Passage to Afghanistan and Bosnia involved individual jihadists. These could be considered mad, bad *individuals*. Passage of British Islamists to Libya and the Free Syrian army was condoned by British intelligence agencies. And yet the departure of young Muslims in groups to fight for IS raised the question of *community* loyalty – or lack of it – in the UK.

Many British Muslims regard themselves as modern worshippers of Islam and they are convinced they are the opposite of the medieval version that is pumped out by fanatics in the Middle East. General Abdel Fattah al-Sisi, the leader of Egypt, has blamed Muslims, especially imams, for corrupting the faith. He said, 'We need a modern comprehensive under-standing of the religion of Islam rather than relying on a discourse that has not changed for 800 years.' In Britain only a handful of the just over 1,700 mosques follow a modernist interpretation of the Koran, whereas in the USA more than half of all mosques describe themselves as adhering to the interpretations of the holy book that adapt to modern life, not the condi-tions in Arabia in the seventh century. In Britain the obviously male-dom-inated mosques make the decisions – perhaps a quarter of mosques do not allow women on the premises, or severely restrict their movements and enforce separate worship. This is not because of the influence of the usual suspect, Saudi Arabia. The Saudis *do* provide money and many of the textbooks for religious schools but the Wahhabis directly control only a tiny number of mosques.

The largest single influence is the Deobandi who control nearly half of all mosques but – far more important – produce the majority of locally trained imams, especially those working in prisons. The Deobandi have always been viscerally anti-British; the cult was created in the Raj around the time of the Mutiny. They enjoyed a close relationship with the Wahhabi movement in what became Saudi Arabia. Deobandi religious debates today are often legalistic and sometimes centre around minor social matters of whether believers should wear ties, even to work, or compromise with Western dress in general, or how many miles a woman can travel, even to a mosque or hospital, without a male guardian. I found one lengthy debate about the pros and cons of whether it was *haram* to wear a bra most enlightening. Maybe Britain should take a leaf out of Norway's policy of trying to ensure that every migrant or asylum seeker takes a course on women's rights.

Reforming Islam is obviously primarily a matter for Muslims them-selves but there has been very little change – as President al-Sisi noted – in 800 years. Indeed the Islamists do not want to go forward, they want to go backwards – to the seventh century. Some Muslim reforms look back not to the time of the Prophet but to the Golden Age up to the twelfth century. It is not entirely true to say Islam missed out completely on the Renaissance,

Enlightenment and industrial and technological revolutions which have produced Silicon Valley. One of the foremost triggers of Western advance was Johannes Gutenberg's mass printing technique developed in the 1450s. It took 400 years for moveable type to come into general use in the Middle East as the Ottomans punished book printing with death. Islam and modernity were not always enemies or even strangers. Before the fall of Baghdad to the Mongol hordes, and before the emirates in Spain were conquered, Christendom was very backward compared with Islamic achievements in the field of literature, law, geography, science, astronomy and medicine – and even cookery. It has been argued that Islam enjoyed a minor period of enlightenment spurred by Napoleon's conquest of Egypt, as well as reforms in Iran, but it was snuffed out by the regressive dictators encouraged by the Anglo-French rulers that followed after the Great War.[2]

A very controversial modern reformer has been Ayaan Hirsi Ali. Born a Muslim in Somalia, she underwent female genital mutilation and a forced marriage (her family says an arranged marriage) before fleeing to the West. In Holland she rapidly progressed from cleaner to MP and ended up teaching at Harvard, married to one of Britain's most eminent historians, Niall Ferguson. She worked on a film with Theo van Gogh who was assassinated by a Moroccan refugee, living on Dutch state benefits, who also threatened to kill Hirsi Ali. She now lives under twenty-four-hour protection. She recently wrote a powerful book called *Why Islam Needs a Reformation Now*. In it she argues that many moderate Muslims are sickened by the atrocities committed in their name. She advocates getting rid of the concept of Jihad, Sharia law and ending the death cult that puts a premium on martyrdom to reach paradise. Hirsi Ali says that women are leading the reformation and that is why Islam has produced Malala Yousafzai as well as Caliph al-Baghdadi. Hirsi Ali has been condemned for leaving the faith and for needlessly inflaming Islamic sensitivities such as saying for example, 'When a *Life of Brian* comes out with Muhammad in the lead role, directed by an Arab equivalent of Van Gogh, it will be a huge step.' Whether she becomes a Muslim Martin Luther or another victim on an IS chopping block is an open question. She believes that a

Muslim reformation will succeed in only some areas, just as the Protestant revolution seduced only northern parts of Europe. The Internet, she has argued, will do for the Muslim revolution what the printing press did for the Christian reformation.

The dramatic reforms Hirsi Ali advocated are unlikely to be enacted any time soon, because even Muslim reformers hate her, not least for her apostasy. Practising British Muslims such as Sara Khan have advocated less radical changes, via her Inspire programme which works on counter-terrorism.[3] Yet she too has been attacked for toadyism because she supports the government's Prevent programme.

The government can enact minor reforms itself, ideally with Muslim majority support, but without waiting for Muslims to reform themselves. For example, welfare abuse. The right wing doesn't like white welfare scroungers either but the regular evidence of Islamist abuse makes the issue more sensitive. The recently jailed British-born Anjem Choudary is a well-known radical 'hate preacher' who managed for years to stay just on the right side of the law – he had trained as a solicitor. He is locked up but his message is not. Choudary used the example of another well-known preacher, Abu Hamza. He lived in a large house with five (of his eight) children – all five were convicted of serious crimes – all on state benefits. The legal fees to deport Hamza cost in excess of £3 million and that does not include the time and expenses of the intelligence agencies. Some of Choudary's acolytes and followers appeared to have no source of income except state benefits. Choudary referred to jobseekers' allowance as 'jihadi-seekers' allowance'. Two of the men investigated in relation to bombing attacks in Paris and Brussels used housing benefit money that Birmingham city council paid (in error) to a jihadist who was actually fighting in Syria. Muslims are often encouraged to lie to unbelievers, especially if a higher moral cause such as jihad is involved. Most Muslims – just like most Christians or Hindus – do not abuse the welfare system. But money paid in good faith for housing or child allowance etc. should not be misused to fund jihadist wars *against* Britain. Such regular well-published abuse – for example by the sex and drug grooming gangs consisting almost entirely of Pakistanis – provide recruiting sergeants for the growing indigenous right wing in the UK, who take up 25 per cent of Prevent energies, compared with 75 for Islamism. One of the right-wing taunts which went viral on the Internet said this:

A Muslim asks his mother, 'Mama, what's the difference between democracy and racism?'

Mother, dressed in her burkha, says, 'Well, son, democracy is when the UK taxpayers work hard every day so that we can get all our benefits: free housing, free health care, free education, grants to build our mosques and community centres, and so on, so forth. That's democracy'.

'But, Mama, don't the English taxpayers get angry about that?'

'Sure they do. And that's what we call racism!'

Louise Casey, the government's 'Integration Tsar', issued a report in early 2017. It said that many Muslims have cut themselves off from the rest of Britain with their own housing estates, schools and television channels. At the same time Sir Michael Wilshaw, the departing chief inspector of schools, warned that 500 schools in England were either 100 per cent white or 100 per cent ethnic minority; pupils in the latter were at risk of alienation and radicalisation. He was particularly concerned about a cluster of twenty-one schools in Birmingham, many of them primaries with no white children. Nearly half of them were judged 'less than good'. Sir Michael also warned of the unregistered Islamic education centres. He also talked of problems with home schools. Ofsted inspectors have no right to report on home schools or their curricula.

A simple answer? Maybe all Muslim faith schools should be closed. Maybe the French model should be adopted and *all* faith-based schools funded by the state, including Christian and Jewish ones, should be axed. If parents want faith education let them pay for weekend classes. This would be glaringly unfair to the numerous Catholic and Church of England schools in what is still nominally a Christian country, especially when no

Methodist fundamentalists have ganged up with masks and AKs, or no Anglican bell ringers or zealous church wardens have formed armed militias, or no provisional wing of the Catholic Church has called for a crusade to regain the lands once controlled by the Vatican in Italy.

Radicalisation problems in schools are often worse in universities where academic authorities are so engulfed in political correctness that they allow gender-separated audiences to listen to hate preachers who should not be in the university, or in the country, for that matter.

In the universities of crime and now jihadism – the prisons – the situation is acute. Up to 70 per of Muslim prison chaplains are from the Deobandi sect. Asking them to curb radicalisation in prison is like inviting Jimmy Saville to run a primary school. Currently out of a total general population of three million Muslims, jails in England and Wales hold around 12,500 Muslims, which is three times higher than the national average. Either Muslims are less law-abiding or the courts are prejudiced. In America the Muslim prison population is eighteen times what it should be proportionately. In Britain roughly 130 Muslims are serving time for terrorist offences, including Anjem Choudary. He is regarded as one of the most dangerous Islamists in custody. The Muslim chaplains often completely fail to curb extremism – many inmates are radicalised or converted while in prison. So the only solution was to take most dangerous radicals and put them in special containment units in three more isolated high-security prisons. Over forty officers have been moved in to control prisoners such as Choudary as well as Michael Adebolajo, one of the two killers of the British soldier Lee Rigby in 2013. He has used his notoriety to recruit others to the jihadist cause. About twelve top terrorist convicts were initially isolated so they could not go on conversion crusades in prison. This is a good start but the authorities should get rid of all the Deobandi chaplains – they have been brought up to hate everything that is British.

The Islamist attack at Westminster in March 2017 by a British-born man, converted in prison, prompted rapid reforms. A 100-person new counter-terrorism task force was set up to deal with the Islamist crisis in British prisons. Ian Acheson, a former senior officer in what was once called Her Majesty's Prison Service, recently led an enquiry into the problem. Unlike most senior civil servants and ministers in the Ministry of Justice he did know very well what the inside of a cell was like and how to deal with tough prisoners who did not want to be inside one. Acheson summed up the nature of radicalisation perfectly:

> Prison is an ideal environment for the death-cult ideology of Islamist extremism to flourish. If you confine violent, credulous and impulsive young men hunting for power and meaning with charismatic and psychologically manipulative extremists, you have the right ingredients. Add in the grievance narrative that is the IS trademark, a dash of conspiracy theory, and lace with the glamour of extreme violence and you have the perfect recipe for Islamism.

The prison service is generally in free fall and can't cope with wider problems such as drugs, drones and violence, let alone radicalisation. Previous fears of being labelled racist and inadequate training have undermined counter-terrorist efforts. Also, the intelligence agencies have been too efficient sometimes by nabbing jihadist plotters upstream and therefore some offenders do not end up in high-security prisons but in less intensive regimes and for shorter sentences. In my own experience of trying to help the Justice Ministry I have come across profound ignorance about radicalisation.

Most of the solutions are obvious, besides kicking out all the radical imams and finding people who can read the literature to stop the dangerous stuff getting in. Separate centres within high-security prisons for extremists are in place and working. Now good staff members are required to control them, Prisons rarely have enough staff to organise catering and exercise for normal inmates. Many are scared of prisoner violence and so the absentee rates for officers are high. The prisons are grossly underfunded and criminally understaffed so finding specialist officers for jihadists will be tough. On April Fools' Day the former failed fusion of the prisons and probation service was renamed Her Majesty's Prison and Probation Service. As Acheson noted, 'This pig is going to need an awful lot of lipstick.'

****

The question often arises – and not just among fascist nut jobs in the pub – why do all Islamists and also many Muslims hate Britain so much? Why do they not go to live in their homeland or join IS? At least some of the radicals had the courage of their convictions and risked Syria, unlike many of the hate preachers like Choudary (who claimed he was prevented from the *hegira* to the IS). It's a bit like the famous Monty Python sketch in the *Life of Brian* arguing about how bad the Romans are:

> Reg: All right... all right... but apart from better sanitation and med-
> icine and education and irrigation and public health and roads and
> a freshwater system and baths and public order... what *have* the
> Romans done for *us*?
> Xerxes: Brought peace!

Dame Louise Casey has advocated various ideas to improve cohesion. For example, getting new immigrants to swear an oath to respect British values and these would be explained, not least about religious tolerance. A new oath may have to be taken by public office holders to uphold tolerance of those with different faiths and beliefs. Instead of spending millions on leaflets in Arabic, Urdu and Hindi etc. the emphasis should be on arranging classes for English, especially for mothers and grandmothers who may be stuck at home and are unable to communicate at all in the country's language. Councils should examine whether their housing policies are contributing to ghetto formation.

You can't force people to live in integrated areas, especially as white flight usually exacerbates this segregation. The government can insist on a minimum standard of English for new migrants, however. Nor can you force people who are already here to speak English or attend classes. Many don't want to – many hang on to the dream of returning home – even over generations. They simply don't want to be contaminated by the decadent lifestyle of the English as they slouch towards Gomorrah. That is why they send their sons to find 'pure' girls as brides in the villages of rural Pakistan or Bangladesh.

Allison Pearson, a well-known columnist for the *Daily Telegraph*, had a lot to say about the Integration Tsar's findings.[4] She noted that the German Chancellor, Angel Merkel, had said that wearing the burqa should be outlawed 'wherever that is possible. A completely covered woman has almost no chance of integrating herself in Germany.' Merkel may be right about this but it goes against the grain of British libertarian traditions to tell people what to wear. Except for specific cases such as customers in banks or employees in public institutions such as schools and hospitals, people should wear what they want. Ms Pearson, well-known for her feminist views, said:

> Let's shut the sharia courts, which count a woman's evidence as less than a man's and often give fathers custody of their children in defiance of what sharia judges like to describe as 'secular' law. Or the law of the land, as we call it.
>
> Over the years, it's been amazing to watch the ethical knots enlightened people tie themselves in as they seek to justify appalling sexist, misogynist or simply illegal behaviour. Just so no one can accuse them of racism. God forbid you should object when a 14-year-old is taken out of school and flown 'home' to get married to a rapey, 46-year-old uncle. Any qualms about such charming imported customs mark you out as 'Islamophobic', a word that turns oppressors into victims.

The columnist also commented on the scale of immigration that has been too big for many communities to absorb, especially in housing, schools and hospitals, which the Casey report also emphasised. While only 13 per cent of the population was made up of foreign-born nationals in 2011, in 2014 27 per cent of births were to foreigners born outside the UK.

This reluctance to integrate, whether on cultural or religious grounds, or perhaps the sheer inability to leave the house or speak English, encourages electoral fraud. Harvesting and fixing postal votes has become endemic in some Asian communities, and not just places such as Bradford, where tribal leaders in places such as Kashmir can have more say than local politicians, white or Asian. Unless someone is temporarily working abroad or provably bedridden then, if people cannot be bothered to walk, hitch, bus or cab to their local polling station or can't read enough English to decide which politicians they have been to told to sign up for, maybe they shouldn't get a vote at all. Besides, Islamists argue that voting in elections is *shirk,* forbidden because it is based on man-made, not Allah's, law. Nobody said integration was going to be easy.

Elsewhere in the book I have tried to be optimistic when I can, although by nature I tend to be a pessimistic cynic. Many books have been written on dealing with Islamic communities in the West, by Christians, Muslims and atheists. I have been critical of how the British government has behaved and how Muslims, moderate and radical, have responded. So far I haven't discussed the charm, grace and goodness I have enjoyed – in war and peace – with Muslim friends. Omar Saif Ghobash is not a friend but I have thoughtful Muslim friends very much like him. He has written a beautiful book called *Letters to a Young Muslim*, addressed to his two sons.[5] He asks how moderate Muslims can find a voice that is true to Islam while usefully engaging in the modern world, and also avoiding theocratic fascism. He writes with an openness that is unusual from someone from such a conservative Saudi-influenced background. He is a cultured man, educated at Oxford, with a Russian Orthodox mother. Ghobash has sponsored literary prizes; his day job is the UAE ambassador to Moscow. He asks why the role models for today's young Muslims is an Islamic warrior, not an architect, mathematician or trail-blazing scientist. He blames much of the narrow-mindedness of modern Islam on the narrow lives of preachers or social leaders rather than the faith. He looks not so much to the seventh-century Arabia but the open-mindedness of Baghdad in the ninth century, Córdoba in the tenth or Cairo in the twelfth and Fes in the thirteenth. He asks why 70 per cent of modern Muslims cannot read or write. He attacks self-censorship and the traditional Arab reluctance to address difficult social, political and sexual questions. He says this is infantilising – just as Arab leaders have infantilised their followers by praising lazy anti-Western shibboleths. Despite his Saudi background, he is tolerant, diverse and cosmopolitan, everything that Wahhabi Saudi Arabia is not. Ghobash's letter on why Islam should be a religion of peace is very moving. He is at his most compelling with his simple comment: 'Knowledge does not consist simply of answers. Great knowledge consists of being familiar with the questions, the doubts, the possibility that things might be different.' This is a truth worthy of all times and all faiths. The British Army encourages 'courageous restraint' on the battlefield, especially in war zones such as Afghanistan, that dictate understanding of the proverbial hearts and minds. Ghobash's book should be read by everyone who is concerned with the tragedies of the Middle East because he shows such courageous philosophical restraint in his letters to the sons he obviously loves so much. This book is an important antidote to the throat-cutting rhetoric of the jihadists. It provides so much hope.

Chapter 6

Dealing with Russia

President Trump promised to do a deal with Russia before the US Navy bombed Assad's air base on 6/7 April 2017 following the regime's gas attack on its own civilians. The Russians warned that the Americans were within a whisker of a direct military clash with their forces. A renewed Cold War could turn nuclear by accident or design and destroy most of the planet rather more quickly than any greenhouse effect. So how should Russia be interpreted?

Russian history can reflect nearly all the sweeping interpretations of how nations behave. It depends, however, partly on where you are standing – in snowbound and besieged Moscow or Washington D.C. on a balmy Sunday when the cherry blossoms are in season, for example. Is ideology important? Yes, because once upon a time communism was going to sweep the world. The great man theory has validity too or, in the case of Catherine the Great, the great woman theory. Sometimes they might coalesce as in Vladimir Lenin's secret journey to Petrograd's Finland Station, kindly arranged by the crafty Germans because the goatee-ed Russian revolutionary called for immediate peace with Berlin. An even older historical tradition maintains that geography shapes politics – hence geopolitics.[1] Russia is vast, the biggest country in the world, and much of it is inaccessible and frozen. In particular, imperial Russia suffered because of its lack of a warm-water port; old-fashioned thinking maybe, but still relevant today.

To the West the Russian bear is often perceived as ferocious when not hibernating. The bear is an apt symbol of Russia – majestic, yet unpredictable when woken up. From the Bear's perspective the West has usually been aggressive. The massive barrier of Siberia in the east has protected that flank, but the north European plain has afforded a convenient invasion route for the Poles, the Swedes, the French under Napoleon, and the German army – twice.

Just as one man's terrorist is another man's freedom fighter, so too Russia's defensiveness based on hard experience may be perceived by an American general as instinctive aggression. The British Army tried to teach its new officers to understand the action-reaction cycle of modern warfare. In 1972 Peter Vigor helped to set up the Soviet Studies Research Centre at the Royal Military Academy, Sandhurst. I found his lectures illuminating and even persuasive, though they were not supposed to indoctrinate any open-minded young second lieutenants. Based on his own experiences of Russians in the Second World War, Peter would deliver a lecture as if he were addressing Soviet officer-cadets at the famous Frunze military academy in Moscow.

He would talk about the mass Russian casualties of both world wars, the abiding fear that the Western allies would forge a separate peace with the Germans. Peter would throw in the acute humiliation of the Brest-Litovsk treaty that Berlin imposed in 1918. A reminder that the intervention in the Russian civil war was an attempt to strangle the Bolshevik revolution at birth would follow. Russians could be trusted, said Commissar Peter. Stalin kept his word to Churchill by staying out of the civil war in Greece and the politburo pulled out of Austria as Stalin had promised before he died. Nevertheless the West helped the fascist West Germans to re-arm. The Moscow-led Warsaw Pact was established six years *after* the North Atlantic Treaty Organisation was founded, and only when West Germany had joined the American-dominated alliance. The CIA stirred up all sorts of revolts and sedition in peaceful Eastern Europe. Meanwhile, the imperialists waged war on many progressive Soviet allies throughout South America, Africa and Asia. Regarding Cuba, it was only Soviet good sense that prevented an all-out nuclear exchange in 1962.

Peter Vigor's chilling ventriloquism lasted till the early 1980s. His legacy was continued in the occasional contrarian thinking at the British Defence Academy/Shrivenham and later the Advanced Research and Assessment

Group (ARAG) which was curiously abandoned, allegedly for lack of funds, when the second Cold War emerged. (Some of the ARAG members continued to participate even when the Ministry of Defence stopped paying an attendance allowance and then removed all travel expenses – a very British method of bureaucratic euthanasia.)[2]

A latter-day Vigor would say that Moscow showed great restraint when the (first) Cold War collapsed. Force was not used anywhere, though Soviet/Russian intelligence played a part in setting up a popular front in Romania after the gory death of one of the nastiest of the dictators, Nicolai Ceauşescu. Even in the heartland of the previous world war, the Soviets withdrew from East Germany on the understanding that it would not be absorbed into NATO. They insisted that the Americans promised that the newly enfranchised countries of the Warsaw Pact would not join NATO. They all did, as did the Baltic states, which had been part of the USSR. Moscow was encircled by enemy forces. As Russian generals used to say, 'NATO forces in Estonia are just a short bus ride [100 miles] from St Petersburg.'

In the West, it is often forgotten that the Red Army did most of the heavy lifting in destroying Herr Hitler, losing 20 millions of its combatants and civilians in the process. Stalin saved Britain from likely defeat. The general view among Russians is that their motherland has saved Europe from barbarism and enslavement many times: from the Mongols, Napoleon and Hitler in the past and now, in 2017, from the Islamic State and other bloodthirsty jihadists. It was only Vladimir Putin who shook the tree in Syria and kick-started the beginning of the end for the head-choppers in the so-called caliphate.

The Soviet Union, however, turned out indeed to be 'Upper Volta with nukes', a vast Potemkin village. Lenin and Co. prophesied that Western capitalism would collapse because of its own internal contradictions, yet the USSR imploded instead. Few Sovietologists in the West saw it coming, perhaps because of constant misperceptions of the Russians themselves, made more opaque by the generally closed nature of their society. It is true that Vladimir Putin has dramatically increased the defence budget but

Russian military spending has been on average one-tenth of NATO's while their economy is one-twentieth, smaller than Brazil, Italy or Canada.

Maybe the West should have been nicer to the bankrupt forlorn country when it disintegrated under the drunken leadership of Boris Yeltsin. Although Russian membership of NATO was discussed, no strategic plan crystallised to bring Moscow in from the cold. Whether Russia – especially under an early Putin – would ever have joined is a moot point. Washington did not offer any kind of Marshall Plan 2 or praise the country for its bloodless revolution. Instead Moscow was smothered by a blanket of American hubristic triumphalism. Just a tiny dose or two of Yankee paternalism could irritate European temperaments, especially the British and, of course, the ever-touchy French. The Americans sent earnest if naïve young graduates from the Harvard Business School and its like to teach the poor benighted Russians how to privatise their industries and how to embrace the glories of capitalism. According to Paddy Ashdown, a thoughtful former Royal Marine, ex-spook and leader of the British Liberal Democrats,

> The result was a bonanza of corruption, the humiliation of the Yeltsin years and a clumsy attempt to expand NATO and Europe right up to the Russian border. There was always going to be a consequence of this folly and its name is Vladimir Putin.

The rise of Putin
How did the sense of closure, even the alleged 'end of history' in the early 1990s, become Cold War Mark 2, possibly more dangerous than the first version?

Putin's Russia meant a reversion to type – one-man ruler, the personalisation of politics. After serving two terms in power (2000-8), Putin – a former lieutenant colonel in the KGB – handed over to his protégé, Dmitry Medvedev. The Russians dubbed this a *rokirovka,* the castling move in chess; Western experts used the term 'tandemocracy', though there was little democracy, especially when Putin castled again to take back the presidency in 2012. More liberal Russians had begun to think of themselves increasingly as Europeans rather than citizens of a highly personalised kleptocracy. Putin had no ideology or civilian project to offer his people beyond revived military strength, beefed up with old-time nationalism and religious orthodoxy. This is what Stalin had done when the Germans reached the outskirts of Moscow. Yet even the fearsome Stalin had men like Marshal Georgy Zhukov who could temper his monomania. Putin did not have a politburo. He has ruled alone. Putin is uniquely unilateral.

Wealthy Russians rushed to buy up smart apartments in London while their homeland retreated into a fortress Russia partly as a result of Putin's military adventures. Disputed parts of Georgia were recaptured from the Georgian army in 2008. Opponents of Putin compared this with Hitler's march into the Rhineland in the 1930s. The highly efficient grab of the Crimea and other parts of eastern Ukraine were the equivalent of Hitler's seizure of the Sudetenland. Or perhaps the comparison could be made with Britain protecting the Falkland Islanders in 1982, except that in Ukraine the compatriots were next door. It was conjectured in the West that the final move into the Baltic states would parallel the Nazi invasion of Poland that triggered the Second World War. Western sanctions were imposed on Russia, which increasingly looked east, not just to China but to forge a Eurasian customs union with some of the former Soviet Republics. The Eurasian Economic Union (EEU) was officially launched on 1 January 2015. Meanwhile Moscow deployed its hybrid warfare – a clever mix of force and deception called *maskirovka*. The Western penetration of Ukraine – encouraging membership of the EU and especially NATO – was a provocation too far to the new breed of nationalists ruling in the Kremlin. Kiev, the Ukrainian capital, had been the historic embryo of the Russian soul. That was the romantic side; more practically, the industrial regions of Ukraine contained crucial defence production facilities. Ukraine itself was an artificial construct created by various border changes (1922-54) which pushed the country farther west. It did, however, gain more territory than it lost, especially to the Russian Federation in the east.

After what Putin described as a fascist coup in Ukraine, Russian intelligence stirred up insurgency in the areas heavily populated by ethnic

Russians. Putin's tactics were infiltration with soldiers – usually special forces in non-Russian uniforms (nicknamed 'little green men') – plus loads of weapons, including the Buk anti-aircraft system that probably shot down the civilian Malaysian airline Flight MH17. Always denying responsibility for the fighting in Ukraine with a straight face left Western governments unsure how to respond. Sending in too many weapons and trainers to the pro-Western government in Kiev might have provoked a more overt occupation in eastern Ukraine, thus establishing a land bridge with the Crimean peninsula. Russia now had the Crimean naval base of Sevastopol, formerly on lease, now part of Russia proper, and, finally, complete control of a warm-water port. (Though there were restrictions on military vessels passing through the Ankara-controlled Turkish Straits.)

The collapse of the USSR and the subsequent two wars in Chechnya had demonstrated the operational deterioration of the Russian armed forces. The savage fighting against the Islamist and national causes in the Caucasus displayed the brutality and indiscipline of the ordinary Russian infantry, though the elite forces did better. In 1999 Moscow dramatically sent an armoured column to block Pristina airport as NATO forces moved into Kosovo. I happened to be with the British forces that first encountered them. The Americans had ordered the advancing Brits to destroy the column, but British General Mike Jackson refused, saying that 'I am not about to start World War Three'. Instead the British had to feed and water the Russians. I spoke to rather bedraggled Russians who showed me inside their armoured vehicles – they looked like museum pieces. In the rush they had not had time to bring much spare clothing. They chatted in their dirty vests while some of the uniforms were drying on a makeshift line hanging between their vehicles and nearby trees.

The short 2008 war with Georgia also exposed Russian deficiencies. Since then Putin has poured money into the defence budget, including new equipment, for example the Armata main battle tank, which is arguably the best in the world. Their operations in Ukraine and Syria indicate that Russia's forces are now much more capable. They have also modernised their precision-guided weapons and their command and control systems. The revitalised Russian forces had fought weak opponents in Georgia. The Ukrainian forces were poorly trained, ill-armed and demoralised. The Syrian rebels, both Islamist and more secular, had often fought with determination but they did not possess an air force, navy or advanced land warfare systems.

The strategic thinking in the Obama White House was channelled through the prism of Russia's ailing economy which was further enfeebled by Western sanctions and the drop in the oil price. Putin's military bravado was perceived as a front to rally domestic support in a country going down the economic tubes. As Barack Obama put it, Putin was 'pursuing nineteenth-century policies with twentieth-century weapons in the twenty-first century'.

Russia had given up on integrating with the West; Moscow would focus on the post-Soviet Eurasia. Strategic ties with China would be built up, while Western influence would be minimised. This trend was exacerbated when general economic sanctions imposed by the EU and America were tightened to include specific companies linked to Putin's inner circle.

Tensions grew with the West over more than sanctions. In Syria both Russian and American militaries tried to manage de-confliction of aircraft. Nobody wanted accidental dogfights. In Europe, aerial brinkmanship was reaching dangerous levels. Russian warplanes were constantly buzzing Western jets – both civilian and military. One of the most serious incidents happened on 7 April 2015: a Russian Su-27 (NATO designation Flanker) flew very close to an American RC-135 reconnaissance plane in international air space over the Baltic Sea. Washington went though diplomatic and intelligence channels to complain about the highly unsafe behaviour but Moscow said the American aircraft had been flying with its identifying transponder turned off.

Shooting down of planes could have led to accidental war between Russia and NATO. Yet some co-ordination over Syria and attempted peace talks and occasional truces as well as airspace management meant that both Washington and Moscow had to talk sometimes. Even more crucially, the two adversaries continued to work on constraining Iran's nuclear aspirations. Also, Washington still needed Russian rockets, not just to send Western astronauts to the international space station, but also – it was not played up in the media – to launch American military satellites. The US could eventually build its own rockets again but it was cheaper to use Russia's ageing though reliable rockets. It suited big financial interests in both countries to maintain this eccentric connection.

Putin continued to rail against the West not just over sanctions but also for failing to stop the Islamic State and sometimes even to blame Washington for instigating Islamist opposition to President Assad of Syria. Most sensitive to the ex-KGB colonel, who had studied German at university, was the threat from Europe. From Putin's historical perspective, NATO was a capitalistic tool that was starting to occupy Moscow's 'near abroad'. Putin warned that sanctions were a part of

the policy of containment... [which] has been carried out against our country for many years, always, for decades, if not centuries. In short, whenever someone thinks that Russia has become too strong or independent, these tools are quickly put into use.

Putin deployed the 'fortress Russia' argument to bolster his own popularity. Defending the Russian people in neighbouring states, especially in Ukraine, galvanised domestic support in Russia. The return to the homeland of Crimea was especially popular among ordinary Russians. The peninsula had been formally annexed in 1783 after the hated Ottomans had been defeated in battle. It had been given to Kiev in 1954 as a token gesture by President Khrushchev to celebrate Ukraine's integration into Russia 300 years before. The defence of Russians and Russian speakers in eastern Ukraine was a big crowd-pleaser inside Russia. According to opinion polls – not all government-sponsored – Putin's rating averaged around 85 per cent, a figure that Western politicians could only dream about. The decline in living standards, partly caused by sanctions, appeared not to influence the President's poll ratings very much. Around 14 per cent of Russians thought that the government should take measures to get them lifted. Regular majorities in polls showed that the EU and, especially, America were considered hostile and deploying a variety of propaganda and physical threats. For example, the sporting bans on Russian athletes because of doping were considered the West's own brand of hybrid warfare.

If not sending sportspeople to the Rio Olympics was a blow to Russian prestige, the geopolitical threat was still paramount. The West simply failed to fully comprehend that dangling EU membership in front of Kiev was seen as an inevitable precursor to NATO membership. This was a red line for Putin. The continued eastward march of NATO was what prompted his famous warning:

> Russia found itself in a position it could not retreat from. If you compress the spring all the way to its limit, it will snap back hard. You must always remember this.

A future war with Russia?

After a successful year of fighting in Syria – namely saving President Assad from collapse – by the end of 2016 Putin looked as if he were on a roll. An admirer, Donald Trump, had even been elected US commander in chief. Putin was accused of deploying Russian cyber power to hack into the emails of Trump's Democratic Party rival, Hillary Clinton, as well as other senior Democrats. Moscow had also improved relations with key Western allies in Egypt, Turkey and even Israel. Moscow started to plan joint naval patrols with the Chinese and then raised the stakes by talking about restoring bases in traditional allies such as Cuba and Vietnam.

Before the advent of Donald Trump it looked almost as if Moscow and Washington were sleepwalking towards a shooting war. Sir John Sawyers was the former head of Britain's Secret Intelligence Service (SIS) – more popularly known as MI6. He warned:

> We are moving into an era that is as dangerous, if not more dangerous, as the Cold War because we do not have that focus on a strategic relationship between Moscow and Washington.

The old protocols of deterrence had been lost. They were not speaking the same diplomatic language anymore. MAD – Mutually Assured Destruction – had been fully understood, and feared, by both initial superpowers. Then China created a triangle. The diplomatic dance became more complicated when rogue states such as North Korea went nuclear. Nevertheless, from Moscow's first nuclear test in 1949 until the collapse of the Soviet Union the language of mutual deterrence had been fully comprehensible – especially during the eyeball-to-eyeball Cuban missile crisis of 1962. After the Berlin Wall was torn down and the USSR dissolved, the Russian Federation maintained most of its nuclear arsenal. In the Budapest Memorandum of 1994, however, Ukraine agreed to give up its nukes – it had the world's third largest stockpile – in exchange for guarantees of its territorial integrity and independence. Belarus and Kazakhstan signed the same protocols which were guaranteed by Russia, the USA and Britain. France and China signed rather more evasive guarantees. When today NATO members look at Russia's covert invasion of large parts of Ukraine, they sigh and say under their breath: 'Thank God, Ukraine is not in NATO or we might have to defend it under article 5.' Yet it could be argued that under the Budapest Memorandum at least America and the UK are obliged to defend *all* of Ukraine. Neither Washington nor London would do much more than send in a few infantry weapons and trainers to avoid inciting Moscow to seize all of eastern Ukraine.

The crisis in Ukraine was testing the mettle of the West. Even a presumed accident, when a Russian anti-aircraft system was sent to rebel-controlled Ukraine and returned within twenty-four hours, could have provoked a very major European crisis when Flight MH17 was shot down with 297 passengers and crew on board. NATO was not treaty-bound to engage in Ukraine but it was in the three very nervous Baltic countries. Would Putin trade on the weakness and disunity in the West and chance his arm by a swift move into the Baltics? Logic would dictate that he should consolidate his position in Ukraine before moving on the Baltics or even into non-NATO states such as Moldova. Putin was rewriting the international order, both in Europe and in the Middle East. The massive migrant crisis connected the two, not always accidentally. Moscow could only benefit from the turmoil in the EU as populism and immigration swamped the attention of the Brussels elites.

What was the mood in the Baltic states? Over one million ethnic Russians live in the three small countries with equally small populations, especially in the cities. Lithuania had around 5 per cent, while Latvia had 27 per cent and Estonia 24, according to the most recent census. Some Russians, and Russian speakers as a mother tongue, felt genuinely estranged by what they regarded as official discrimination but not all of them wanted Russia to intervene. Many enjoyed the freedoms that Estonia, Latvia and Lithuania had to offer as EU members, not least to travel and work throughout Europe. Many of the 'Russians' tend to live in the cities. In Riga, the Latvian capital, around 50 per cent are native Russian speakers, including its first ethnic Russian mayor since independence.

One way to gauge how the vast majority of *non*-Russian inhabitants feel about being ruled once more by Moscow is to visit the former KGB headquarters in Lukiškės Square in the centre of the Lithuanian capital of Vilnius. It is an imposing neo-classical building with thick walls that were useful for absorbing the screams from the many previous torture victims. Thousands of Lithuanians were shot here. It is now called the Museum of Genocide Victims and it describes how a third of the country's population were killed or deported to Siberia, courtesy of their Soviet liberators who had driven out the Nazis. The Germans used the building as an HQ in the Great War and then the Gestapo took it over in the second great conflagration. I have spent some time in various museums in the three states and they all seem rather coy about how many local inhabitants shared the Nazi hatred of the Jews and failed usually to describe the large number of often eager recruits to the *Wehrmacht* or SS.

Just like young Israeli conscripts who are taken to Yad Vashem, the Holocaust museum in Jerusalem, so too young Lithuanian soldiers are taken to see the barbarities of Russian rule. The Baltic states have endured a very short but cruel history. The non-Russians would fight hard against a Russian invasion but they cannot do so without help.

Moving into the Baltics may well prompt war with NATO. Probably, but not certainly. It partly depends on the old Marxist term – 'the correlation of forces'. After the collapse of the USSR – which Putin referred to as 'a major geopolitical disaster of the century' – the nuclear arsenal provided the crutch for dramatically deteriorating conventional forces. By definition, this reduced the threshold at which Russia would consider the use of nuclear weapons. Russian military strategists talked more openly about the usability of nuclear weapons, as the Americans had in the Dr Strangelove era of the 1950s and 1960s. One Russian hawk talked publicly of 'reducing the US to nuclear ash'. Conversely and paradoxically, Putin's massive revitalisation of his conventional military capability could have the advantage of *raising* the nuclear threshold. Equally, the major decline in both American conventional commitments in place as well as languid European defence spending must mean that NATO will have to resort to doomsday weapons sooner rather than later if a shooting war breaks out with Russia. Or just surrender.

NATO members wondered whether Putin was mad enough to swallow the Baltics, which he could do in days. Or was it all a bluff? Appearing slightly crazy can be useful in terms of military deterrence. It is conventional wisdom that North Vietnam waited for the departure of Richard Nixon prompted by Watergate in 1974 before they overtly invaded the south. They thought that the domestically besieged Nixon might be dangerous enough to throw everything at them for breaking the Paris Accords (and meanwhile looking tough to disenchanted American voters). Likewise, it was often said that French nukes had more credibility because President Charles de Gaulle was belligerent enough actually to use them. And today the great leader in North Korea may well be mad and bad enough to fire his nukes, if truly threatened – though it is often joked that anyone given that kind of haircut would go nuclear.

Whatever his clinical state – and Putin did not appear to be in even the same hospital let alone psychiatric ward as Nixon or Kim Jong-un – the Baltic governments have been extremely worried. Lithuania reinstated conscription. It also issued its third survival guide since 2014. It is a seventy-five-page pamphlet offering advice on how to recognise friendly militaries and how to deal with unfriendly nuclear or chemical attacks. The Latvian national guard has been on constant red alert and many kept their weapons at home in readiness for the attack they feared was imminent. Estonia has hidden 1,000 large survival capsules in their forests with supplies to support two years of guerrilla resistance. Noir dramas about Russian occupation played on Scandinavian TV. Russian media started showing civil defence preparations and old nuclear bunkers. And, in a sad display of British impotence, Boris Johnson, the UK foreign secretary, declared that people should protest outside the Russian embassy in London. That would strike fear in the heart of Putin, obviously. One solitary protestor with a single placard turned up. Most successful leaders know when to stop – many warlords display hubris, or overreach as it is now called.[3] Hitler was the classic example, though he was probably insane. Appeasement, that noble flowering of liberal thought and logical legacy of millions dead in the trenches, would have worked with a rational German leader. Would appeasement work better with Putin or is he the classic bully of Western media characterisation who has to be confronted?

If Russian forces drive over the border into the Baltics, swamping the three small countries in days, it would present NATO with an existential threat to the organisation and the West. If, at the beginning of the inevitably swift invasion, the diverse national ambassadors to NATO actually managed to agree on the declaration of Article 5 – 'the one for all and all for one clause' – as happened after the abomination of the onslaught on the Twin Towers, then what? Victory in Cold War Mark 1 depended on the belief that America would save its European allies. To recapture the Baltics would require a replay of Operations OVERLORD plus DESERT STORM. Such a conventional assault – assuming NATO could eventually summon the will and capability – could go nuclear. In the 1960s Charles de Gaulle never thought that the US would risk sacrificing Washington to defend Paris. Washington is increasingly disengaging from an alliance which has become one huge welfare state, where America carries over

70 per cent of the load; the European states are largely freeloaders and dole-merchants who scrounge from the system.

Novels often get closer to the truth than official histories. A former NATO deputy commander, General Sir Richard Shirreff, has written a controversial novel called *2017 War with Russia*.[4] This is only a slightly dramatised version of intelligence dossiers and war games that amount to a *cri de coeur* about Western, especially British, defence cuts. Russia invades Latvia, Estonia and Lithuania after stirring up the Russian minorities and then paralyses NATO by threatening to launch nukes. Shirreff's point is whether the West could pre-empt invasion by putting sufficient conventional defence forces into the Baltics or in nearby Poland. The British general rams home his point by explaining why the biggest ship ever built for the Royal Navy, the *Queen Elizabeth* aircraft carrier, is sunk because it has no on-board fighter aircraft, or accompanying maritime surveillance planes, or enough escorts, both surface and submarine.

The foreword of the book is written by Admiral James Stavridis, the US naval officer who was former Supreme Allied Commander Europe. He said, 'I would put Russia right now as the number one threat … . Russia is the only country on earth that retains a nuclear capability to destroy the United States. That is an existential threat.' He added:

> Yes, jihadists pose a massive threat to our security but, until the jihadists can defeat us on the battlefield they cannot destroy our nation. The Russians are different – and this is the truly terrifying bit – as they appear to be prepared to use nuclear weapons, based on recent, very public comments by Vladimir Putin.

Shirreff's novel has a very senior military crony of the Russian President toadying up to the Boss:

> That is the true genius of your plan, Vladimir Vladimirovich. NATO and the West will think this is about Russian speakers, but it is also about the balance of power in Europe. When NATO fails

to react to our seizure of the Baltic states it will have failed, been defeated, and probably collapse. At that moment it will cease to pose a threat to Russia. Without NATO, Europe will be forced to beg us not to go any further. And apart from eastern Poland, which historically has been part of Russia, we probably won't. We'll be happy to visit Paris as a tourist.

Spoiler alert: if you want to read the novel, skip this paragraph. Although Russian forces take the Baltics easily, resistance is continued in the forests. Western special forces manage to penetrate the Russian enclave of Kaliningrad to turn the nuclear-armed missiles against Moscow, after a very clever cyber attack. The Russians withdraw from the Baltics, and Putin is mysteriously – and conveniently – 'accidentalised' in a helicopter crash.

In real life some of General Shirreff's warnings have been heeded. NATO decided to send four battalions of troops to the Baltics, including one from Britain. A handful of front-line aircraft, such as the Typhoons, have also been sent. Ironically these were originally designed at the height of Cold War Mark 1 to outclass Russian fighters. Then everybody assumed that that role would be redundant. America also appears to be beefing up its armoured reinforcement and more troops have been sent to Poland and Romania.

Despite the American cruise-missile strike in response to a gas attack, Moscow-Washington relations may still find some detente over Syria or in some sort of bizarre Putin-Trump tango; meanwhile NATO is beginning to reinforce its conventional capability to avoid the rapid resort to 'tactical' nuclear weapons. To the West Putin is Vlad the Invader but to even his critics at home he is Ivan the Bearable. It is the first time since Hitler that European borders have been changed by force. Putin is dangerous but he is not apparently mad. Meanwhile NATO must be strengthened, particularly as the EU and especially the euro appear to be disintegrating. NATO is still the touchstone of European, and Western, security.

What to do?

- Maintain sanctions until progress on ceasefire and greater autonomy for eastern Ukraine. The occupation of Crimea, it must be accepted, is a fait accompli (but can still be used as an initial bargaining chip).
- The West steps up its modernisation of the Ukrainian army, but non-aggressively, for example, with better intelligence and communications equipment, and training more soldiers outside the country.
- NATO must re-arm, not least with more tanks, and other mobile armoured forces. Member states must properly adhere to the 2 per cent rule of defence spending, and not fiddle the figures as even Britain has done. The need for British re-armament is discussed elsewhere. Also, European members spend too little and too badly. They have wasted billions on duplication and redundancy.
- The whole point of NATO re-armament is to show the Americans that Europe can share the burden and prevent an isolationist creed dominating the White House. A beefed-up conventional deterrent will mean that the chance of an early resort to nukes can be avoided.
- Develop a much closer military coalition with Russia in the Middle East. Maybe Putin was right about keeping President Assad in power, at least in the interim, as a better alternative to the Islamists and certainly a better option than a revived Islamic State. The West and Russia (and China) have a great deal of mutual interest in containing the jihadists. The nature of possible solutions to Syria and Iraq are discussed in the chapters on the region.

In the end the West must work with Russia, not back Moscow into a corner. Maintaining a tough line on Ukraine, and even more so the Baltics, while working together against the Islamic extremists, could create the grounds for a strategic and not just a tactical relationship. This could stop Cold War Mark 2 becoming the Third World War.

Chapter 7

Wider threats to the West

So far the Russian and Islamist threats to the West's security have been discussed in some detail. Here I want to touch on apparently more peripheral challenges. I have spent a lot time in Darfur which I regard as perhaps the first environmental war of the twenty-first century. Of course politics was involved but desertification has played a big part in conflicts in North Africa. I could also, for example, examine the impact of competition for water elsewhere, not least in Israel and Jordan. I consider the manmade degradation of our air, ground and water as a key challenge facing mankind. I am not scientifically qualified to pontificate on these matters, however, so I will have to disappoint the presumably small minority of my readers of the tree-hugging, sandal-wearing Guardianista persuasion. I want to very briefly discuss two separate but also inter-related issues: China and cyber warfare.

China

I remember visiting Beijing at Christmas time a decade or so ago. The shops and tourist hotels were decked out in Western festive paraphernalia. The most upmarket shops boasted European-looking mannequins, signs mostly in English and Western fashions. The Chinese were obviously developing a successful capitalist economy – for a second the old Russian joke about Brezhnev flitted across my mind: 'with all this abundance it would be such a shame if the commies took over.' Senior communist officials I met seemed rather embarrassed when Westerners like me asked about the great revolutionary leaders of the past. Mao was as long dead as Marx.

In late 2008 I was chairing a Beijing conference on Sino-African relations. I was of the opinion that China was perhaps less rapacious than its

French, British and American predecessors. Africa needed trade, not aid. And China, for all its self-interested greed, was providing just that. Africans liked the way that China had pulled itself up by its own bootstraps and leveraged 400 million fellow countrymen out of poverty. Despite the riots against Chinese traders, notably in Zambia, and the fact that the Chinese were using their power to cherry-pick assets and resources throughout the continent, the Chinese still seemed more appreciated than the former colonialists. As President Festus Mogae of Botswana put it, 'I find that the Chinese treat us as equals. The West treats us as former subjects.' Africa was largely impressed by the rapid Chinese ascent to near or actual equality with American economic power (though China had more than four times the – ageing – population to support with that same GDP).

China's economic and military growth has been so striking that it has often caused kneejerk reactions in the US and Europe. Put simply, two main schools of thought exist.

- The peaceful China. Its new strategic cosmopolitanism is geared to expanding its national interest – not ideology – primarily to secure energy sources and to improve its trading patterns with the EU and US.
- The difficult China. China's outreach is part of an exclusionary policy with illiberal and rogue states. North Korea is the prime example. It develops trade patterns that ignore all human rights concerns. This undermines Western conditionality strategies that aim to improve conditions in autocratic countries, not least in Africa. China could manipulate its vast US dollar surpluses to bring down the American economy, though that would not be in Beijing's immediate interest, particularly when it's stealing Western intellectual property worth tens of billions of dollars, especially by cyber raids.

Chinese foreign policy is sufficiently nuanced – proverbially 'inscrutable' – to allow a variety of interpretations. Washington's policies toward

Beijing contain elements of mutual economic co-operation but also strategies, especially with Japan, that could be perceived by the Chinese as
military threats. The problem is mutual threat perceptions work both ways,
just as Kaiser Bill's Germany felt 'encircled' while its neighbours felt
menaced, or Moscow believes that NATO is encroaching into its sphere of
influence. If a dispassionate reader looked at the numerous US bases that
surround China, you could see why the country – historically a land power
– started building a navy.

China has had a massive population problem. The 90 per cent Han
inhabitants were crammed into the plains of the heartlands. They looked
West as the Americans did. Just as the Iron Horse brought white settlers
to the lands of the Apache and Navajo and other great Native American
tribes, so the new Chinese railways have been bringing the Han to Tibet,
for example. Now there is much to be said for Richard Gere and his fellow
activists; the Himalayan cultures of Tibet especially but also Nepal and
Bhutan I have grown to respect greatly. Personally, I would prefer Tibet to
be independent and see the erudite Dalai Lama ruling in Lhasa. But any
real understanding of China must be contextualised by its long history
of war partly caused by the main invasion routes, from the Mongols to
the century of humiliation when Western powers dominated the country
and then the Japanese raped and pillaged. And the Americans threw their
weight around in the civil war between the nationalists and the commu-
nists. The Chinese have just concerns about securing their borders.

To continue with the American historical analogy, the geopolitical
writer Robert Kaplan expounded the theory that the South China Sea is
to the Chinese today what the Caribbean was to the USA at the beginning of the twentieth century. The Americans, after they had consolidated
their land mass by conquering the Wild West, had become a two-ocean
power (Atlantic and Pacific) and then moved to control the seas around
them, pushing the Spanish out of Cuba, for example, and then endlessly
meddling in much weaker South American countries. Both the USA
and China feel themselves exceptional states – America's 'manifest destiny' and China's variations on the 'mandate of heaven'. One of the few

Americans who fully understands China and is respected by their leaders is Henry Kissinger. In his magisterial *On China*[1] Kissinger makes a number of important points. He says, 'The world order, as concurrently instituted, was built largely without Chinese participation. Hence China feels less bound by rules in the creation of which it did not participate.' He also emphasises the fear that China has of outside powers threatening its periphery and therefore posing a threat to its heartland and its domestic institutions. When China did perceive such threats it went to war – in Korea in 1950, against India in 1962, along the northern border with the USSR in 1969 and against Vietnam ten years later. Some of these threats were very real, not least from the American generals of the time. Some of them wanted to use nukes when Chinese armies overwhelmed the US-led coalition in Korea. It was a close-run affair: America could have used nukes in anger a second time, and only just a few years after the atomic bombing of Japan.

At the time of the Korean War the communist leadership was only one year on from the end of the long civil war with the American-backed nationalists. Today the communist party is in the ascendancy both at home and abroad. After taking over as general secretary of the Chinese Communist Party in November 2012, Xi Jinping has secured his dominance very rapidly and has also flaunted his dominance, though not cultivating a personality cult like Mao's. President Xi has dumped the collective leadership and his grip has been strengthened by an intensive nationwide anti-corruption campaign which appears genuinely popular with the masses. China was always diffident about accepting the mantle of great power; not any more, not least in relation to the USA. The massive economic surge has dropped to 6-7 per cent which is still humbling for the Western growth rate, especially in the EU. In 1981 the Chinese economy accounted for less than 3 per cent of the world output; now it's about 18 per cent,

Both Obama's so-called 'pivot' towards Asia and Trump's plan for a 350-ship navy have been designed to check China, especially as it is seen by Washington and its Asian allies as a threat, not least in the South China Sea. The Chinese were mightily offended by Trump's early conversation with the Taiwanese president and the suggestion that the US would go back to the two Chinas policy. (There are of course *four* Chinas; besides the mainland and Taiwan there are Hong King and Singapore. But that is another story.) The US arms Taiwan to the teeth and would probably go to war to defend it – unless Taiwan declared independence. This would destroy Beijing's myth of One China, and probably prompt a reciprocal declaration of war by Beijing. The whole US-Beijing-Taipei diplomatic tango is based on a hypocritical myth. But it is a convenient myth that, so far, has prevented war. Trump's provocative attitudes regarding Taiwan as well as the withdrawal from the Trans-Pacific Partnership trade deal have disturbed the region. Part of President Xi's new assertiveness is his personal assumption of the position of military commander in chief after a shake up of the general staff. He has given himself operational control of the Chinese nuclear trigger. The Chinese president has also congratulated himself on the unveiling of the country's first homemade aircraft carrier as opposed to a pimped-up ex-Soviet rust-bucket. China is way behind the US Navy but its advanced ground-based missile systems could play havoc with an American fleet that came too close to the mainland and China's fighter aircraft are capable and plentiful.

North Korea

Trump's erratic diplomacy had disturbed America's friends, especially Japan and the Philippines, but then his robust stance towards North Korea and by implication China reassured them. China's multiple transformations of reefs and rocks into naval and air bases in the South China Sea and grandiose claims of territorial waters have upset especially the Philippines but also neighbours such as Vietnam and Malaysia. The ratcheting up of tensions over North Korea was also a major flashpoint. Trump's people may just be tempted to deduce that if Beijing won't pull the plug on the Kim dictatorship then American firepower might have to do it before North Korea's arsenal can reach the continental USA. Taiwan remains a potential erupting volcano unless some of Trump's more level-headed diplomats can assuage Beijing.

On the other hand, Trump could surprise the world by offering China a dramatic deal over North Korea. Beijing is frequently exasperated by North Korea but tolerates it partly because it doesn't want the country to collapse and create refugee mayhem. Nor does it want US and South Korean forces to advance to the Chinese border. Trump could be unortho-dox enough to offer China unopposed control of North Korea – 'liberated', perhaps, while the baby-faced dictator is on a special (and rare) medical trip to Beijing. Everybody would benefit, not least the terrorised and starv-ing citizens of the country. The US would promise to keep South Korea in check. Re-unification might have to wait for ever but anything would be preferable to Kim Jong-un triggering a nuclear war. Such a Machiavellian triumph for Trump diplomacy seems highly unlikely, of course.

If China's absorption of North Korea is unlikely, then what else can be done? This question is something that Trump has inherited after a long history of failed US policy planning. Washington has tried talks and pres-sure plus secret plans to destroy the potential nuke programme. Now the rogue country has nuclear weapons and just possibly the ability to reach the US homeland. The 'nationalists' in the Trump camp – epitomised by Steve Bannon – wanted a lot less active foreign policy. Bannon has been demoted and the generals, especially Mattis and McMaster, have had a much freer hand. They could be described as globalists perhaps. Obama kept his generals on a tight leash during his era of 'strategic patience'; Trump is not a patient man and his defence strategy in business had always been to attack hard and fast first if threatened. How does that relate to people like Kim Jong-un?

It is possible to argue that the young dictator in Pyongyang is at least as rational as Trump and certainly more consistent in what he wants. Previous sabre-rattling has led to talks with the big powers, including Washington. North Korea wants to be regarded as a normal state but on its own terms – as a nuclear power treated with respect. Daily for decades magazines, books and TV documentaries have predicted the fall of the isolated state. The regime in Pyongyang wants to make clear it is here to stay and to dis-abuse its enemies of the notion that regime change will make everything better. There are no easy options to deal with the country. It may be possible to take out the nuclear infrastructure by heavy and pinpoint bombing but this could spread dangerous contamination. Even if North Korea does not or cannot respond with its nukes, it will certainly attack South Korea with its numerous conventionally armed planes and artillery. Seoul is just thirty-five miles from the border. It is not a border of course but a DMZ – a demilitarised zone – marking the ceasefire line of the war that *paused* in 1953. No peace has been brokered – this is a long ceasefire and it could soon be broken.

It is important to understand North Korea's origins. The ruling party derives from the small group of partisans who were trained by the KGB, and later the Chinese, to fight the Japanese army which occupied Korea from 1910 to 1945. It was born in Japanese brutality and it still responds brutally to threats. Its rogue status is not just because of nuclear weapons. It produces and smuggles currency and narcotics on an industrial scale. It has a vast small-arms industry. I spent a year or so investigating its involvement with arming the Tamil Tigers for my book on the war in Sri Lanka. It has energetic spy rings around the world, sometimes kidnapping people to work in the hermit kingdom, most infamously to help its film industry. It has conducted well-known assassinations, most recently Kim Jong-un's half-brother in Kuala Lumpur's international airport. It stifles even the mildest internal dissent ruthlessly. There may be up to 120,000 political prisoners in horrific camps. Ideologically it is in some respects the last hold-out of Stalinism. Despite all the apparatus of a communist party, it is in fact a Neo-Confucian feudal kingdom run by a dynasty now in its third generation. Even Stalin did not try to elevate his son as heir. And yet the dynasty is not completely secure – the power behind the throne is the military. The hard-line generals naturally support the state philosophy of military first. They are committed to the unification of the peninsula, by any means. Nukes help here. Also, as the regime looks at the downfall of Colonel Gaddafi it concludes that he and Saddam before him might have survived if they could have wielded the threat of atomic deterrence.

In short, the regime leaders may be bad but they are not mad. There is method in their over-the-top rhetoric about frying their enemies. The Chinese are their sole friends and only play at sanctions for Beijing's international image. The Chinese pretend to stop coal imports going north or oil going south. Washington stopped any hints of Taiwan or South Korea going nuclear but as late as 2012 North Korea was publicly parading huge Chinese-built missile launchers in Pyongyang parades. Even if Beijing decided to cut the life support it may be that the North Korean military would not listen to China and replace President Kim if he looked like making a deal with Beijing, or especially Trump.

Washington wants China to take the lead, and also Moscow which has some, but far less, influence. That is the problem with letting a rogue country develop nuclear weapons. It is probably too late to use military power against Pyongyang. In that sense, North Korea has won. They have behaved dangerously but not insanely.

*****

Trump made a diplomatic gaffe when he launched his first act of war when President and Mrs Xi Jinping were visiting the so-called summer White House in Florida in April 2017. The Chinese leader will have hidden it but he must have felt affronted by being involved – no matter how accidently – in such a dramatic assault not just on President Assad but also on Russian prestige. It was also a dent to Chinese pride, unless Trump took the very unlikely precaution of *fully* briefing the boss of the Chinese Communist Party. American diplomats have tried to spin the probable insult to the Chinese president by suggesting that he was privately rather impressed by Trump's macho stance. Unlikely. They talked trade but many potential powder kegs surround the two presidents, besides North Korea.

Accidental conflict in the South China Sea is a more likely trigger to real fighting talk. The Pentagon has sent a number of planes to fly in what China claims is restricted air space. And soon after Trump took over as president, an aircraft carrier strike group, led by the USS *Carl Vinson*, was sent to the South China Sea to demonstrate its sea lanes are open to international trade. Trump's literary claim to fame is his book *The Art of the Deal,* which was entirely ghosted. The Chinese general Sun Tzu wrote the *Art of War* more than two and a half millennia before. It would be foolish to underestimate the Chinese.

Cyberia

The Chinese have made themselves masters of war in cyber space – or 'informationalised warfare'. The current heroes, or anti-heroes, of this genre are people like Julian Assange and Edward Snowden. Snowden's story might have been made into a Hollywood movie, but he was a traitor who has done massive intelligence damage to the West. Despite the praise of female London luvvies and the John Pilgers and Ken Loaches of this world, Assange has managed to make a fool of them all, and cost them a lot of bail money. As right-wing columnist Douglas Murray put it,

> what they have is a teenage anarchist whose sole political development over four and half decades of existence has been to move from his mother's basement into the back room office of the world's largest exporter of bananas.

Cyber warfare is the new fifth domain – after land, sea, air and space. Cyber threats are probably of greater concern to the West than even Islamist terrorism – it is not just a question of targeting command and control of armies, or switching off Predators, or guidance for tanks; it is economic too. The massive cyber assault on 100 countries in May 2017 turned off many vital IT systems in Britain's National Health Service, for example. It is possible to knock out power grids, too. The Russians turned off the electric grids in Ukraine in December 2015. The power failures accompanied Moscow's simultaneous illegal military operations in the country. The Russians dubbed it Operation SANDWORM. The Russians also managed to close the Georgian government website during their war in 2008. Moscow's proxies also hacked the Warsaw stock exchange as well as a French TV station. The North Koreans have about 3,000 top computer scientists working for Pyongyang (compared with about 400 South Korean equivalents). The North Koreans hacked Sony Pictures in 2014 – revealing lots of embarrassing emails – apparently because the company made a comedy about the country, and especially its batty leader, called *The Interview*.

The West has been busy too – the US is probably still the leader in cyber warfare capability. In 2003 the Pentagon took over the Iraqi networks and, inter alia, sent emails to various generals advising them to surrender. Famously, US intelligence services worked closely with friends in Israel to deploy Stuxnet to cripple the Iranian nuclear programme. Obama also authorised the tapping of his good friend Angela Merkel causing her to liken the US National Security Agency to the Stasi, the former East German secret police. Whether Obama also authorised the tapping of Donald Trump has been strongly denied by US spooks and GCHQ in England. In the past the UK has done a number on Americans when USA intelligence was forbidden to do so by law. That was a while ago, apparently.

Most US presidents are identified with a war during their time in office. George Bush Junior, like Tony Blair, will always be damned by the Iraq connection. Donald Trump models himself partly on Ronald Reagan who presided over the end of the Cold War. Pundits predict that Trump's conflict will be the Korean War Mark 2. Others predict that his buffoonery might trigger the Third World War. Some experts suggest that he is at war already – a cyber war.[2] The alleged Russian hacking of the Democrats is supposed to have tipped the election in his favour. Yet the Russians can be fair-weather friends. The Internet abounded with comments about Putin's alleged 'buyer's remorse' when Trump hit back at Russian interests with the cruise missile strike on Assad's air force base.

Cyber hacking used to be a hobby for the bedroom-bound supergeek, then it became a major criminal activity involving millions of minor and major hacks into companies, many of which remained unreported. Most electronic penetrations are for commercial reasons; the Chinese commit an immense amount of intellectual theft. The military applications for cyber warfare are also immense. The US set up its Cyber Command in 2010 to co-ordinate its attack and defence capabilities. The problem is that no protocols are agreed. During the Cold War arms control arrangements and hot lines etc. created a complex matrix of restraint and mutually agreed mechanisms to prevent accidental nuclear war. What if someone hacked into the command and control of nuclear weapons systems?

Maybe we should all become Luddites and go back to a simpler age. Sometimes spooks or even Foreign Office officials have resorted to using pen and paper if they are operating in a dodgy cyber environment. It may also be possible to use manual systems to operate power grids. Modern war fighting is based on C4ISTAR.[3] To be completely safe, computers, including smart phones, will have to be ditched. With the rapid advance of artificial intelligence, the malevolence of cyber space – and the dangers of a computer takeover of the world – becomes a real concern, not just sci-fi. Isaac Asimov's three rules for robots may become three rules for humans. Do not own a computer, do not use a computer and never power one up. Try semaphore instead.

Chapter 8

Future Options

Quo vadis America?

'The press takes Trump literally but not seriously. Voters take him seriously but not literally.' So wrote US writer Salena Zito about the 2016 US election. It was this paradox that helped the Donald to win. Trump was once considered a Democrat and then he wanted to stand as a Republican presidential candidate but his new party didn't want him to be a candidate. He doesn't really fit into any formal political category. Maybe Trump himself doesn't know – he acts on instinct. Perhaps the best definition is that he is the first independent nationalist president since the nineteenth century. At the inaugural ball in Washington it was fitting that Trump chose the Frank Sinatra hit *My Way* as the song for the first dance. And he wants to make America and the rest of the planet dance to his tune. He gazed at all points of the compass and saw that the world needed Trump.

In contrast, many Americans wished a plague on both candidates because the choice was so bad. P.J. O'Rourke, the famous satirist, was also famously Republican but he admitted to endorsing 'Satan', Hillary Clinton. 'Better the devil you know than the devil who knows nothing ... Better *bien-pensant* than *pas de pensées*.'

Nevertheless, for good and bad and by accident or intent, Trump looks like changing the world in a number of ways (if his own advisors, Congress and Supreme Court can't stop him). He disparaged NATO but then – fairly – said that Europeans should pay their way (although presenting Angela Merkel with a big bill was not the most diplomatic way of achieving this). He offered to make friends with Putin, if he could. The American cruise-missile intervention in Syria might interrupt play for a while, however. Trump had doubts about free trade deals that have stripped US workers of jobs and seemed to be opting for much more protectionism – the traditional response of US isolationists. Initially he appeared to be ditching the One China policy established decades ago. When he was a candidate he said that the agreement Obama (and other major states) made with Iran 'was the worst deal I have ever seen'. And yet he has not so far ripped up the deal. He also castigated Kim Jong-un as a 'bad guy' and hinted that countries like Japan and South Korea could gird themselves with nukes so as to deter Pyongyang. In addition, he said that if Beijing did not rein in North Korea, then America might have to do it alone. Then he said he was prepared to talk to President Kim and President Trump sympathised with the job Kim had done after being forced to take over his father's reins while being so young. Nor was the Donald a fan of the Green movement – he said he would cancel the Paris Climate Agreement. Aid would be downsized as well.

Trump has portrayed himself as a hard power kind of guy. He increased the defence budget by $54 billion (which is bigger than total UK defence spending). In theory this would buy 60,000 soldiers, 12,000 US Marines and another 100 combat aircraft. And the US Navy would expand from 274 ships to 350. The Royal Navy currently has nineteen major ships so you can estimate the different scales between US and European contributions to Western defence.

Thus far, Trump's foreign policy instincts are arguably less provocative than Hillary Clinton's strategy would be. The Donald did promise 'to kick the shit out' of IS but his actions have been measured, so far. Maybe he is listening to a few old hands. At one level the president is running a solo tweetocracy, which drives the self-important White House press corps utterly mad. Trump the showman has largely ignored not just the Fourth Estate but also the 'fourth wall': he speaks directly to the audience, like an aside to camera on TV or in the movies or theatre. No longer do the established media have to mediate between ruler and ruled. The presidency can never be a solo act, however. Trump has gathered some able people around him, especially the generals – he seems to like straight-talking tough guys in uniform. Among these alpha males in the White House the British son of a Hungarian dissident, Dr Sebastian Gorka, has been given a high media profile. Regarding IS, Gorka said:

> We're here to win this war. ISIS can be crushed. I reject this meme that has been propagated for years now, that this is a generational war. We can not only destroy ISIS; we can destroy the entire brand of jihad. Churchill was right – you never go to war unless you define your victory.

Gorka works in a sort of strategic think tank inside the White House team that focuses on long-range planning. He reported directly to Steve Bannon, Trump's chief strategist (and Svengali to the Washington press corps), Reince Priebus, the chief of staff, and Jared Kushner, the husband of Trump's daughter Ivanka. They all seem to think and act differently. Trump, however, seems to think family first. In the disputes between Bannon, in the nationalist camp, and Kushner, more a globalist, Bannon came off worse and was demoted.

The new secretary of state was a surprise appointment. Rex Tillerson, a former CEO of ExxonMobil with no previous diplomatic experience, said his wife convinced him by saying God wanted him to do the job. Presumably even the Donald would agree that God is a much higher authority than himself. Tillerson admitted his surprise at being offered the job by Trump, whom he had never met before.

The generals he has appointed are very smart and not yes-men. The most celebrated is General James 'Mad Dog' Mattis, the new defence secretary. He is almost a walking book of (his own) quotations. He meets and greets some people with his famous lines which he is said to have used in Afghanistan, 'Do not cross us. Because if you do, the survivors will write about what we did here for 10,000 years'. Another well-known warning is, 'I come here in peace. I didn't bring artillery. But I am pleading with you, with tears in my eyes. If you fuck with me, I'll kill you all'. Another quote worthy of a fighting general was his classic antidote to Dale Carnegie's method of winning friends and influencing people, 'Be polite, be professional, but have a plan to *kill everybody* you meet'. As the commander of the Marine Division in the 2003 invasion of Iraq he led from the front; during the push on Baghdad he relieved a colonel of his command for not advancing fast enough. He is said to be a scholar as well as a warrior. The general carried a copy of the *Meditations* of Marcus Aurelius with him in Iraq and Afghanistan. Personally, I am a little suspicious of these extrovert classicists. Lawrence of Arabia took classics in ancient Greek with him into battle, and he was certainly weird. The few modern versions of this type I have met in war zones are also a bit strange, whether they are classicists or they have learned the Koran by rote.

Mattis has been a hawk on Iran; Obama sacked him from Central Command because of his hard-line views on Teheran. The new Secretary of Defense does not want to tear up the Iranian deal, which was patiently negotiated over years, though he would be prepared to come down hard on Iranian breaches of the agreement. General Mattis is also keen on curbing Iranian proxies, especially the potent fighting militia that is Hezbollah. The anglophile general is certainly not soft on Russia or China, as his 2015 testimony before the Senate armed services committee indicated. Mattis might help to tone down Trump's electioneering statements – not least on the utility of torture, which the general opposes on various grounds.

General H.R. McMaster took over from the hapless General Michael Flynn as the national security adviser. He too is a scholar-warrior who wrote the respected book on Vietnam, *Dereliction of Duty*. This doctorate-turned-book is a savage indictment of the dishonesty of civilian leaders as well as military chiefs; this work could easily have been a career-stopper. In addition, he is reputed to be a brilliant strategic thinker. Trump *et al* might need such a man because some believe that America has become like Germany after Chancellor Bismarck was ousted in 1890. War has become a bad habit for Washington, even under Obama. There is a view that McMaster can restore a Clausewitzian balance, that military strategies can be subordinated to a grand strategy.

We have been here before. Unlike the Old World, Americans often have displayed a touching faith in their generals' genius despite their many (sometimes obvious) flaws. Numerous examples offer themselves in the Second World War; more recent examples have been highly able but flawed officers such as Generals David Petraeus and Stan McChrystal. Twelve generals made president, starting with George Washington and ending with Dwight Eisenhower. In contrast, it is very rare for serving or recently serving officers to achieve real political power in Britain in modern times. Lord Kitchener was an exception as well as, to a lesser extent, Jan Smuts, a South African general. A British historian teaching at Harvard, Niall Ferguson, has said of the group that Trump has recruited from, 'Never in the history of the English-speaking peoples has there been an officer class this good.'[1] Even if the Scottish professor is correct, I still hope they don't get the chance to lead the West *into* another major war. Their job is to keep us *out* of wars.

Not only does Trump like generals, he likes the military pomp. He wants to be seen around the aura of military power. The president beefed up military operations in Yemen and then around Mosul and Raqqa. So far, his biggest surprise was the US cruise missile strike on the Syrian air force base at Shayrat which allegedly launched a major chemical strike on civilians in Idlib province. Obama consulted with allies and Congress before finally backing off from hitting Assad for crossing the chemical red line. The Donald did not consult with anyone outside his inner circle, though he did warn the Russians to get their personnel out of the way of the fifty-nine cruise missiles. What is Washington's new policy for Syria, however, beyond some sort of return to regime change? If the IS leadership were prone to bubbly, they would have been opening their best captured stock. Bombing Assad's forces is a diversion from the main effort against the caliphate.

Opponents of Trump banged on about him being a second Hitler and that his populism was repackaged and modernised Nazism. Despite sharing a very bad haircut, Donald is not another Adolf. A better comparison – though still a stretch – is with Kaiser Bill; the Second Reich works better than the Third. Trump is dangerous not because he has evil intentions but because he is impulsive and erratic, like Kaiser Wilhelm II. Bill liked generals as well but he could not work out a coherent policy to utilise his army, probably the best in the world. He would bluster and pose; Trump is obviously good at this too. His first press conference as war leader was on 7 April 2017 where he took on the role of a solemn generalissimo. Trump is a great actor, perhaps almost as accomplished as the American actor who brilliantly satirises him, Alec Baldwin.

Russia

Predictions about Russia are always difficult at any time. A few years back who would have predicted that Russia would dismember the Ukraine? At home, barring a plane crash, it can be safely assumed that Putin will stay in power for the next six years after predictably hobbling his main political opponent, Alexei Navalny. The president wants total control and it is all about making Russia great again; it is all about respect. One of Britain's most eminent experts on Russia, Professor Robert Service, summarised Putin thus:

> Putin lacks Lenin's ambition for world revolution and is no communist but he is smitten by a fondness for the Soviet decades when Russia successfully projected its power far beyond its borders. He is convinced that the Americans have unjustifiably barged into countries such as Iraq and Libya which had once been under the USSR's influence.

Putin epitomises the deep streak of sentimentality that beats in many Russian souls. For hundreds of years, for example, many Russians wanted to recapture Constantinople to make it Christian again. Putin's realpolitik has enabled Moscow to improve relations with Ankara, despite Turkey shooting down a Russian fighter over Syria in December 2015. Domestically, Putin has shown a great interest in not only reviving Tsarist history but also the position of the Orthodox Church. Putin has become a sort of puritan Che Guevara advocating a conservative-religious idealism both at home and abroad. He has defined Russia as a moral bastion against sexual licence and decadence, porn and gay rights. Despite his authoritarianism, the old cruelties are much reduced. Under his gangster style the occasional opponent is murdered but the Katyn massacres, say, or the legions sent to the gulags have not been repeated.

The fact that Trump, without having met Putin, should pour such effusive praise upon the Russian autocrat is worrying and yet the American Commander in Chief has promised to deal openly with his Russian counterpart. The blow to Russian prestige by the big US cruise missile attack on Assad's air force in April 2017 might be overcome if it is a one off. Trump is also said to want Russia to use its restricted influence on North Korea. Moscow would want a reduction in sanctions on Russia for starters. That might mean a decline in tension. It was obviously Lady and the Trump from the cold treatment that the US president handed out to Angela Merkel on their first formal meeting in Washington in March 2017. She might do better to concentrate on her working, if not warm, relationship with Putin – they can both talk freely in Russian and German. The Russian appears to respect the German leader.

In this year of the centenary of the Russian revolutions, Putin could sit back and enjoy watching the decline of the capitalist EU. He does not want complete chaos but would estimate that EU weakness, especially if the euro collapses, is likely to undermine NATO. Trump has backtracked on his initial disrespect for the alliance. And his new defence secretary and secretary of state plus the US vice president have done much during European visits to reassure nervous EU leaders. And yet the ideological core of Trump's advisors respects Putin as a leader because of the way he has stood up for his country's interests. They believe – perhaps rightly – that Russia is entitled to be the dominant power in its own backyard. That is a match for the US Monroe Doctrine regarding America's near abroad. Also there is a realisation that Russia has a measure of justification in its arguments that it was treated badly after the end of the first Cold War. And the more historically minded among Trump's inner team say they want to avoid a repeat of Germany and Versailles. A mistreated Russia was bound to seek revenge. It is probably too late to redress that mistake, however. Perhaps also the macho posturing of Putin, in his topless fashion, appeals to some Trump people, and presumably Trump himself, who appears to model his facial expressions on another dictator, Benito Mussolini. The millions of hits on the Internet of a photo-shopped topless picture of Trump riding on the back of a horse also mounted by a topless Putin, looking just like Dobby the house elf, has aptly satirised the strange bromance. The Internet also parodied Putin's alleged Faustian pact with Trump:

> Twinkle, twinkle little czar
> Putin put you where you are.

On a more serious note, it is often suggested that the rise and fall of liberalism in Europe has had a lot to do with Russia. Post-war liberalism, on both sides of the Wall, was partly sustained until 1989 by the Soviet menace. Remove it and Europe reverts to type – quarrelsome populism and nationalism. A renewal of the Russian threat may be the only way of keeping the EU and NATO alive.

The Russian tide may not yet have turned. The threat to the Baltic states has been examined in depth earlier in the book. Moscow is also busy meddling in the Balkans. Serbia, traditionally a Slav ally, may decide to revert to Moscow's embrace especially if the EU implodes. Moscow has been accused of an attempted coup in Montenegro. The small but strategically important state is the only country on Europe's Mediterranean coast that is not in NATO. It is seen as the last piece of unclaimed real estate between Lisbon all the way to the Syrian port of Latakia. Many unresolved tensions still bubble away in Kosovo, Albania and Bosnia, all states which have been the source of a large number of jihadist migrants to the Islamic State.

Putin has dramatically improved his standing in Russia and abroad, making lots of powerful geopolitical friends. He ignored Obama on Syria, and got away with hacking away at the US elections and yet originally appeared to have seduced Donald Trump. Even at the height of Soviet power the idea that Moscow could try directly to influence an American election would have been unthinkable. Putin has played a weak hand very well. He has snubbed the US not least in the Middle East and projected his power in Europe, despite a declining economy. Sanctions have made Russians much poorer than before the first intervention in the Ukraine. But much of this imitation of the old USSR, like the original, is all smoke and mirrors. The undersize, smoke-belching aircraft carrier that played a role in Russian military domination in Syria says it all, not least compared with the vastly bigger and far better US carrier fleets. Putin succeeded in Syria because America stood back and let him. Obama had talked tough but acted soft. Arguably, US vital interests were not at stake in Syria or in Ukraine. Putin will try to co-opt the Trump administration, not least in the final endgame with the IS. Regardless of the possibility of a Trump-Putin compact, Moscow will almost certainly avoid goading a potential friend in Washington by moving immediately into the Baltics. And yet Moscow's hybrid warfare deliberately blurs the boundaries between war and peace meaning that military mobilisation can begin long before any (unlikely) formal declaration of war or actual military incursions that would be tantamount to war. Take the case of Russia mounting cyber attacks on Latvia plus manoeuvres involving around 40,000 Russian troops on the border which were exercises. Next time it could be real, however, and the US president might decide initially that an invasion is just fake news, especially as he seemed initially reluctant to listen to – or even talk to – his own intelligence agencies.

The logical conclusion is that Putin should sit back and count his blessings. But that is not often the way of successful dictators, is it?

Britain and Europe
Britain

The BBC has regularly been accused of pro-EU bias. *Spectator* columnist Rod Liddle noted that the Beeb's reporters looked horror-struck when it eventually dawned on them the morning that Brexit had won the 2016 referendum. He wrote, 'The presenters and reporters looked magnificently shocked on 24 June as if they been touched up or, in some cases, violated by a gibbon.' To be fair, so did Boris Johnson, the chief Brexiteer. Few in America expected Brexit and certainly not Obama, who promised to put Britain at 'the back of the queue' if it went independent and tried to sort a free trade deal with Washington. The special relationship generally floundered under Obama. It was always vastly overvalued in the UK when Britain's ego was politely stroked, at best, by most US presidents, even during the Blair-Bush love-in. In contrast, the anglophile Trump promised that Britain would be at the front of trade deals with the US.

The unelected Brussels bureaucrats richly deserved Brexit and the British electors were right to give it to them. If Britain had stayed out of the Great War, and thus saved millions of lives, then Germany would have dominated Europe earlier. Admittedly, it would have been rather Prussian to start with, but the virus of Nazism would not have been hatched. There would have been no Treaty of Versailles to inspire revenge, no Hitlerian 'stab in the back'. Millions of Jews would not have been gassed. Europe would have evolved pretty much as it has today: a German-dominated trading bloc still making good cars and tanks. The British decided to leave the EU for many reasons – dislike of Germany, except on the football field, was not one of them. Sovereignty of Westminster and uncontrolled immigration were the important factors. As in Germany in 2016 and in Britain some time earlier, ordinary voters felt that the political parties were not listening to their concerns that things were getting out of control, not least in housing, schools and the health services. Mass migration has always been as much a social danger as a political one. Brexit, however, was not a vote to reverse immigration but rather to *control* it.

In Britain it is possible to argue that racist and xenophobic *politics* have never been weaker. Yes, the police – partly because of changes in the way such offences are recorded – have observed an increase in anti-Semitic as well as anti-Islamic incidents. And yet formal racist parties such as the British National Party almost disappeared in the 2015 UK general election. Of course many British remainers regard the UK Independence Party as racist. Theresa May, the new prime minister, said after Brexit that borders serve a purpose. Failure to manage them erodes public confidence and also undermines support for immigration and for helping refugees. Britain wanted to avoid the mass influx of migrants that overwhelmed Germany in 2016.

Trump's promise to build a wall and get the Mexicans to pay for it has been much derided. He has been attacked as racist and nativist. And yet throughout history, from the Romans to the Chinese to the Israelis, successful states have done this. This is what European states did before, and are doing again now – at least building fences, after a brief utopian Schengen fantasy. 'Good fences make good neighbours', said the poet Robert Frost. And yet in the long run walls and fences can be self-defeating and create dangerous partitions as in Korea or formerly in Berlin or Northern Ireland. For the time being stopping the mass ingression requires physical barriers – and much better policing. Germany has realised that admitting more than a million immigrants in one year – most of them male, Muslim and with no more right to be in Europe than anyone else in the world – has caused many social, political and economic problems in the most successful, and so far stable, state in the EU.

As the earlier discussions in the book suggested, Islamist extremism in Britain has been facilitated by ghettoes created by the disastrously failed policy of multiculturalism. What is the point of continuing to bring migrants into a country that is, especially in areas such as Birmingham, so bad at integrating them? Even if Britain installed a new citizenship oath, what will the authorities do to people who break that oath? The level of immigration in Britain (as well as Holland, Germany and some other European states) has severely weakened faith in integration and in government itself; hence the new populism throughout the continent.

As the three Islamist attacks in England between March and June 2017 showed, MI5 has been overstretched monitoring indigenous terrorists, let alone foreign ones. Until Brexit kicks in, any potential terrorist can seek asylum in Eastern Europe or EU states in Scandinavia and then have the right, after a few years, automatically to live in the UK. Britain has already suffered blowback from waves of Islamists coming home. Some went to fight in Afghanistan and Bosnia, though their numbers were small. Then larger numbers travelled to Iraq. British intelligence agencies often turned a blind eye to those UK Libyans who wanted to fight against Gaddafi, and British Syrians who wanted to remove Assad provided they worked with the Free Syrian Army. Soon London realised its mistake when nearly all the British volunteers in Syria switched to IS or its al-Qaeda-linked rivals.

At least Britain can plan to control its own borders. It can soon say who can live in the UK and if non-citizens break the law, especially by committing terrorist acts, can then kick them out after serving time. Half of the immigrants came from outside the EU and the lacklustre and poorly led Border Force has been slack in enforcement. The Border Force needs to get its act together especially by improving its naval assets. The handful of cutters operating around Britain will soon be beefed up but even more ships are required for the lengthy coastline of the British Isles. MI5 has recently doubled its strength – but the numbers are still too small to monitor all the suspected Islamists (and increasingly right-wing local threats). The Islamic State has promised to send thousands of its warriors to Europe, so the fall of the caliphate is likely to accelerate revenge attacks on the continent and the UK. Many more linguists are needed in the security serves and especially women, who make better and more disciplined watchers (mobile surveillance officers) than their male counterparts, for example.

Talk of defending British borders prompts the questions of *which* borders. Brexit raises awkward challenges in the demarcation between EU Ireland and the non-EU UK. Nobody wants to go back to the bad old days of fences, watchtowers, customs and big queues. Brexit also poses difficult challenges for Scotland: its inhabitants might have to choose *which* union they want or maybe none at all. Nobody expects a new Hadrian's Wall but an independent Scotland raises many acute security questions, enough to fill a book on its own. To mention a few: where will the Trident force and its successor shift to? What of the historical Scottish regiments? And Putin will be more than happy to see northern Britain abandon its air defence systems. The Celts are on the march. If Scotland leaves and Sinn

Féin augments its successes in the 2017 Stormont elections and the end result is a united Ireland, what happens to a stripped-down England, with a reluctant hostage-appendage of Wales? An unlikely scenario now, but possible. On the other hand, if the UK stays united it could return to an older idea: to fulfil Churchill's dream of closer economic, defence and political union with the Crown countries of Canada, Australia and New Zealand. In the (unlikely) event that it worked, the CANZUK union could form a third pillar of Western civilisation alongside the USA and the 'United States of Europe'.

*****

If more Muslim inhabitants of Britain become actively radicalised or passively tolerant of Islamism then more robust state measures many be required. The frequency of terrorism offences has doubled since 2010. Most are home-grown and, also, converts are disproportionately active, as with the Khalid Masood attack in London in March 2017. Converts constitute just 4 per cent of British Moslems but make up 16 per cent of terrorist offenders. Many of the converts are petty criminals who get radicalised in prison. It is no longer like *Porridge*. Wholesale sacking of radical Muslim chaplains should be just the start of the prison reforms before the levels of incarcerated Muslims reach the startling French or American levels. As the death of Constable Keith Palmer — stabbed to death by a British convert in the grounds of the parliamentary estate — indicated, policemen doing such sensitive and potentially dangerous jobs should be armed. Police forces, especially outside London, are short of armed officers, however. One of the reasons for the shortage is potential recruits are understandably deterred by the fact that the Independent Police Complaints Commission insists on treating armed officers as suspects every time they discharge their weapons. Admittedly, some of the armed officers could do with more training. That means more cash. The police's job would also be much easier if the UK finally returns to the previous wartime practice of national identity cards, which some libertarians have resisted for too long.

If the successor to the Islamic State continues to brainwash so many British recruits to commit domestic terrorism, as opposed to joining the jihad in the Middle East, then internment may be a drastic resort. Britain introduced internment in Northern Ireland and in colonies such as Kenya and South Africa. It didn't work well in the colonies and was probably counter-productive in Ulster in its 1971 guise. Its earlier use, co-ordinated with the Irish government in 1956-62, was more successful. Arguably, the largescale American internment of Japanese during the Second World War did work, despite the many individual injustices; and perhaps the internment of some Germans and British fascists at the same time in the UK proved effective, in some cases. Britain interned enemy aliens in both world wars, including a few inoffensive Italian ice-cream vendors. If Britain does ever have to move on to a serious war footing then a whole raft of unpleasant measures, from detention without trial to press censorship, might have to be introduced. Nobody would want that even if the so-called fifth-columnist argument were dangerously valid. In short, adopting a more kinetic policy to destroy IS and the whole jihadist brand – as Trump has advocated – could avoid long-term casualties and domestic authoritarian measures later. Winston Churchill was asked to cut the government's budget for arts during the height of the war but he refused. He asked 'What are we fighting *for*?' To preserve the moral high ground in the battle for ideas it is vital that British domestic values are maintained. Also, it is of course the Islamist strategy to polarise and inflame Muslim opinion in the West so as to boost Islamist recruitment. Most British Muslims already claim they are being discriminated against. That polarisation has happened on a small scale in the UK and to a larger extent in France – with bigger and more regular atrocities on the continent. The only long-term solution for Muslims is to reform themselves, not least to purge jihad as war from their faith, and deal with what is primarily a problem for Muslims – worldwide. All the policing measures in the world are just sticking plasters. Muslims have to clean out the mess in their own religion. But is a Mohammed Martin bin Luther about to ride over the horizon?

The European Union

The EU faces at least two big internal problems: Muslim immigration and the structural future of the Union itself. The 55 million Muslims in Europe could be integrated – if they want that and if the process is slow. The Turkish Gastarbeiter came in and mostly settled in well because of the smaller numbers and the much slower process, plus a determination to fit in. Suddenly the influx is now measured in hundreds of thousands – no society can absorb such a number without significant goodwill and willingness of Muslims to try to integrate rather than establish their own Islamic societies outside the Dar al-Islam.

Fox News was lambasted recently for talking about no-go areas in Europe; yet there is some truth in the story. Large parts of France are effectively not French. Diplomats warn of ungoverned spaces – especially in North Africa – that spawn terrorism; parts of Europe are now almost as ungoverned. Twelve years ago the *banlieues* exploded and over 9,000 cars were torched. Soon the threat fell off the media radar, however. The murder of cartoonists and Jewish shoppers in Paris perhaps wasn't enough of a red light. It took the mass murder of concert-goers, football fans and diners relaxing in Paris restaurants to wake up the authorities. The French have the biggest problems because France has the largest percentage of Muslims per capita of anywhere in Western Europe. It has 2,600 mosques, three of which have been closed down recently because of terrorist activity. Just outside Paris, one mosque yielded 334 weapons, a large quantity of ammunition for AKs and IS propaganda videos. Most Muslims have been placed or chose to live in run-down areas where there are few jobs. Given the density and lack of opportunity, disaffection and then radicalisation are not surprising. In 2012 the French state decided to reassert authority in fifteen areas not just in Paris but also in Lyon, Nice, Strasbourg, Amiens and elsewhere where the population is majority Muslim and where the police rarely went (except in force). In 2014 a leaked French intelligence document warned that Sharia law and Islamic indoctrination were active in seventy supposedly secular state schools.

Next door, in the wealthy failed state that is Belgium, the various competing stovepipes of police and intelligence organisations had given up in the Molenbeek suburb of Brussels, which generated a series of major Islamist attacks on the heart of the EU transport infrastructure. The German town of Dinslaken, which is partly ghettoised, has become a hotbed of radicalisation. The same goes for Dewsbury in West Yorkshire (although the town also produced Britain's first Muslim cabinet minister, Baroness Sayeeda Warsi). And yet France has alienated many more of its citizens and residents well beyond those who actually join or want to join the caliphate. Germany could soon face problems of French proportions, however, as Bret Stephens opined in the *New York Times*:

> Now Germany will have to confront a terror threat that will make the Baader-Meinhof gang of the 1970s seem trivial. The German state is stronger and smarter than the French one, but it also surrenders more easily to moral intimidation. The idea of national self-preservation at all costs will always be debateable in a country seeking to expiate an inexpatiable sin.[2]

Europe's long peace has largely depended upon the presence of American military might. Europe – including Britain outside the EU but still in a modified NATO – will have to learn how to harden its soft power. That might mean, for example, a military return to Libya, to sort out IS there but this time with a bigger and better plan than it has now. It might entail a super-Marshall plan. Facing down Russia might also have to invigorate European purpose if the new American administration of 2017 does not swing some sort of deal with President Putin.

Meanwhile Germany is undergoing a rapid transformation. It's not just that hundreds of thousands of migrants are pouring in. It's that a huge proportion of them are teenage and twenty-something young men. In Sweden 71 per cent of all asylum seekers in 2015 were men. Among late teenagers, the so-called 'unaccompanied minors', the ratio was 11.3

boys for every one girl. Young men are like young men everywhere and all societies with skewed sex ratios tend to be unstable. And the vast majority of these men possess views of women's roles in society that are the opposite of the norms of contemporary Europe. The only solution that will dramatically augment the numbers: these young men will try to find a way of bringing brides and their families to Europe. Men with wives and children are less likely to grope young Christian women in short skirts or spray graffiti over synagogues or indulge in terrorism, although the intelligence agencies are worried about an uptick in the age of terrorists. The March 2017 family-man attacker in Westminster was 52, the same age as another British convert who left his family in Britain and later drove a car full of explosives into Iraqi government forces in Mosul a few months before.

Opposition is gathering momentum, on the right and left, to Merkel's highminded folly in allowing so many refugees. A potential rival in a party in coalition with hers, Jens Spahn, a minister sometimes spoken of as a future chancellor, called for a ban on burqas, niqabs and other forms of Islamic dress that cover women's faces. He said:

> In this sense I am a burqaphobe. Anyone who thinks men are worth more than women, refuses to learn German, or to send his daughter to school swimming lessons should seek asylum in a country that suits him better.

The elections in Europe in 2017 – especially in France, Germany and the UK – have been dominated by the migration and security questions. In Holland in March 2017, the centre-right Mark Rutte saw off the challenge from Gert Wilders, the firebrand right-winger (who increased his number of parliamentary seats). But many of the other Dutch parties appropriated much of the Wilders's agenda, including Rutte's famous warning to immigrants to 'behave normally or leave'. Many other right-wing topics are now on the debating list in Europe's most tolerant country: an end to dual citizenship, a burqa ban, the removal of students' grants at a so-called

Islamic university in Rotterdam, plus wider powers for the intelligence agencies, not least to monitor social media.

*****

It used to be said that the EU was like riding a bike, once you stopped moving you fell off. It may now be more like a 'wall of death' waiting for the spinning cars to lose traction and crash. The momentum has been in the wrong direction for many Europeans and not just the 'insular' Brits. The Union is celebrating its precise sixtieth anniversary as I write these words. Originally it was designed to prevent war and avoid the conflicts that had destroyed the continent. So it was always a vision, a big political project, and not just a trading club, which most Brits thought they were joining in the early 1970s. Then I was an active supporter of that kind of British entry. What has happened is perhaps inevitable. As the memory of the wartime anguish has dissipated by the arrival of new generations, and as the EU institutions grew stale and sclerotic, the system has become less successful. Initially London envied the continent's economic success as Britain was dubbed 'the sick man of Europe'. And yet the necessary domestic reforms, especially curbing the destructive power of union Neanderthals, were forced through by Margaret Thatcher, albeit at much social cost – especially in the traditional coalmining areas where I grew up. As Britain became freer and less regulated, the EU was increasingly constricted by red tape. Then came the single biggest disaster – the adoption of a single currency in 1999 and the mistaken idealism of incorporating all the economically unready countries of southern Europe. The Germans were always going to do well; the euro was a gift that kept on giving, even when Berlin had to bail out the less industrialised and more corrupt deep south, especially Greece. In northern Europe the cultural cliché was of the 'lazy Greeks' while in the south the notion was consolidated of the 'coldblooded Germans who live to work'. An idealistic solution was that the south would have to accept fully 'flexible' labour markets as in the north, while Germans would have to be forced to abandon their 'destructive' saving habits and give up their 'selfish' export-based economy. This Damascene change in mindsets was not going to happen. The 2008 financial crash brought many of the cultural, political and economic tensions to a head. The financial markets began to doubt endless German or EU willingness to act as lenders of last resort to the debtors of the south, and this combined with the fall of interest rates to near zero.

When the EU leaders talked of ever closer union many Europeans did not listen or just paid lip service to the dream. When the Brussels elite talked privately of a real United States of Europe, on the US model, many of the Euro-federalists knew their voters would not buy it. The reality of the disasters caused by the Schengen agreement and the euro brought out all the contradictions of the Union. Besides the catastrophes inspired by Schengen and the single currency, only the most cunning of Putin's agents would have suggested the current matrix of EU government, not least a parliament that switches venue every month at a yearly cost of 180 million euros. Many Europhiles, as I used to be, would put up with the Brussels gravy train because it was always going to be better than war. Now the EU institutions are likely to collapse under the weight of their own contradictions and bring down Europe with them. Britain may not have an EU to Brexit from.

The chief villain was always the euro. It was obviously a case of putting the cart before the horse but the Europeanists assumed the institutions would catch up. Joseph Stiglitz, a top American economist who won the Nobel Prize, was once a big supporter of the EU and common currency. In his recent book, *The Euro: How a Common Currency Threatens the Future of Europe,* he has recanted. He said the monetary experiment is 'an economic and political disaster'. 'Flawed at birth', he argues, 'the structure of the euro is to blame for the poor performance of Europe, its successive crises and increased inequality.' He then proceeds to analyse the repercussions of the obvious point that tying together countries with vastly different economic and social backgrounds denied them the paramount ability to manipulate their exchange and interest rates. The Euro-federalist argument that only more Europe will save the Union will make things worse, like alcoholics arguing for just one more drink before they stop. Stiglitz concluded his book by asserting that Europe may have to abandon the euro to save the European project. It may be too late.

If I were a better economist I would argue, in detail, that the future of the European single currency should be subordinated to a worldwide debate about a new monetary system for capitalism; to consider a post-capitalist order for the twenty-first century. The whole post-war economic settlement does certainly need revision, starting with the International Monetary Fund. The collapse of capitalism has been extensively – and inaccurately – predicted for a very long time. And usually the texts are almost impossible to read, often written by German sociologists.[3] An exception is Todd G. Buchholz's *The Price of Prosperity*. The author is an interesting American polymath, whom I would recommend if his only achievement were co-producing the fabulous Broadway and West End show *Jersey Boys*. He examines why rich nations have failed in history and how they can be renewed. He cites key factors such as falling birth rates, trade deficits, rising debts, eroding work ethics and 'waning patriotism'. Some of his ideas to boost patriotism include wellworn remedies for citizens and new immigrants, such as a form of social and national service on the Swiss model. That won't fly. Another idea is that migrants should have a booklet inserted into their passports which stipulates that the new American or new European has to visit a series of historical sites, museums, galleries etc. to have their extra passport stamped and thus learn something about the adopted country. It is not a bad idea that all new migrants to Germany and Austria, for example, should be asked to visit Auschwitz and similar camps inside the German border.

The future of the Middle East
IS endgame

At the time of writing the Islamic State is shrinking rapidly in both Syria and Iraq. Previously al-Qaeda killed lots of people and captured headlines; IS was different – it also killed lots of people but captured territory. That's why Islamists worldwide were so enamoured. Al-Qaeda had promised a caliphate but now IS had really built one. They were winners. The state is now disappearing and jihadists don't like losers, especially if they appear to be out of favour with Allah. They are quitting, not jihad but the IS organisation.

In Syria IS occupies only one corner of a crowded battlefield. Islamic State's former ally and then enemy, al-Qaeda, renamed itself al-Nusra Front and has since rebranded itself again. It still has about 10,000 active fighters in Syria. And the various other fronts and militias probably can add another 60,000 armed jihadists. All are outside the IS shrinking enclaves. These fighters primarily want to get rid of Assad although the long-term goals, hitting the West and building a more successful caliphate, are the same as IS. Their ambitions are currently limited to the Syrian battlefields; that is why some Western intelligence agencies have tried to court them. So the destruction of IS will not witness the end of aggressive Salafist jihadism; instead the return home of some of its fighters, especially to the West, will cause a spike in terrorism.

Syria currently has four main domestic contenders and none is strong enough to defeat the others, even with the kinetic intervention of their international allies. The groups are the Assad regime, the anti-Assad rebellion which is largely Islamic or Islamist, the Kurds and the declining Islamic State. The Russians and Iranians have been bolstering the regime, which had once helped boost the Islamists (some of whom went on to form IS). Many Islamists were released from Assad's prisons – partly to justify his claim that the rebellion was a conspiracy, both Islamist and foreign backed – and nothing to do with internal demands for democracy. Turkey also assisted IS as a way of bringing down Assad, its regional enemy. Then Ankara switched sides to work with Saudi Arabia and Qatar to back the non-IS jihadists. Washington claimed to back non-Islamists in the Free Syrian Army but they were mostly mythical or, where they existed, were ineffectual – except as arms suppliers to IS. The West's far more effective ally has been the Kurdish-led Syrian Democratic Force, which is dominated by the Kurdish YPG; the alliance also includes some Arab tribal forces. The Syrian Kurds are disciplined and effective; the US had finally found a force that has a rare habit of winning battles in the Middle East.

The YPG – with US special forces and airpower – has done well in fighting IS, most notably in the big battle for Kobani. Yet the YPG has had a tacit alliance with the Assad regime and has sometimes skirmished with US-backed Arab militias. The YPG has also been hit by Turkish artillery, air strikes and ground troops as it moves into northern territory vacated by retreating IS. Turkey is Washington's key NATO ally. Ankara had assumed that IS would keep the Kurds in check but IS foolishly spurned its tacit ally by hitting targets in Turkey. The Syrian Kurds look like emulating their kin in Iraq by carving out a Kurdistan in the north (called Rojava) which would normally drive the Turks mad. Turkey's intelligence agencies and security officials, however, have been totally distracted by containing the aftermath of the attempted coup in Turkey in July 2016. Turkish intelligence people and security police have also been busy ensuring that President Erdogan won his April 2017 referendum to make himself El Supremo. One of the lessons of Afghanistan and indeed most insurgencies is that an adjacent sanctuary is needed to win a successful guerrilla war. IS is landlocked and so it badly needed Turkey for all sorts of resources, equipment, medical back-up and, above all, a conduit for its supporters to travel in and out of its embattled domain.

At the start of the Syrian uprising many opposition people felt they would secure the support of America. The refusal of Obama to directly intervene militarily made the frustrated rebels turn to Saudi and Kuwaiti donors and the failure of Obama to respect his own red line over chemical weapons finally pushed many into the arms of the Islamists. Despite Western liberal perceptions about the Syrian uprising, as with many other misunderstandings of the Arab Spring, the battle cry of every rebel group in Syria was always *Alluha Akbar*. The rebellion, right from the start, was Islamic, and it became increasingly Islamist.

President Trump's first action regarding IS was to send 700 extra US marines to man an artillery section to attack the IS capital, Raqqa. The nearby town of Manbij, towards the Turkish border, is around twenty miles from the Euphrates. It is a mixed town with many Kurds and Arabs plus other minorities. Russian troops were assisting units of government forces there. The Kurds had invited the Russians in, presumably as a hedge against Turkish forces. The Americans were there too, helping to keep the peace between Kurds and Arab militias, presumably with Russian connivance. To add extra layers of complications, the US military was helping the Kurds but the CIA was aiding the Arab militias, so in this area it could have been argued that the conflict was a CIA proxy war against the Pentagon.

The patchwork quilt of different armies and militias was replicated in Iraq. Here the Americans were fighting in tandem with Shia militias, whereas in northern Syria US allies were Sunni Arab groups. In Damascus an Alawite Ba'athist president was still in power, whereas in Iraq the chaos is partly a result of America's toppling a Sunni Ba'athist dictator. Saddam's Ba'athist – largely secular – military intelligence officers were still largely running IS and used to engage happily with their old allies in the Syrian government military and intelligence matrix. The imbroglio was far more complex – here we need to keep it simple, especially if we are looking to predict the future.

The dramatic final Iraqi battle to capture Mosul is a little like the race to reach Berlin first in the Second World War. Just as it was not then simply a case of Nazis versus everybody else, so too in Mosul lots of different interests were jockeying to benefit from the fall of the city. The result of this battle was likely to shape the northern boundaries/borders for the Kurds, Shia and Sunni Arabs, not to mention the various minority groups. The Kurds have given impressive assistance but said they would not enter the city itself. The prize would be manipulated to look as if the small pro-government Sunni militias had done the donkey work, not the hated Shia militias or the more tolerated Iraqi army.

So what happens when the IS finally evaporates? There will no surrender as in a conventional war. Some fighters will flee to Europe, others will go to Libya, or join other jihadist groups in Syria. Some locals will shave their beards off and mingle back into their nearby towns and villages. The fight against Assad will go on, presumably. Iraq cannot be put together – it is humpty-dumpty time and the same is probably true of

Syria. Assad looks like winning – not least by surviving. With his Russian, Iranian and Hezbollah allies he still has the *upper* hand but the American cruise missile strike has shown he no longer has a *free* hand. He could carve out an Alawite enclave, linking the coast with Damascus and might be able to hold it with the help of his powerful allies. Other Sunni Arab parts of Syria could form their own canton. The Kurds will go their own proud way, if they can. Iraq will – has – split into its traditional Sunni, Shia and Kurdish components. Whether Iraqi and Syrian Kurds will put their enclaves together is discussed later when I consider a new partition of the Middle East – one the locals want, not what French or British (or Russian and American) cartographers dictate. The future is cantons, not countries.

IS is older than it appears. Setting aside the prophetic precedents of the seventh century, its near ancestry resides with Abu Musab al-Zarqawi who was an emir of al-Qaeda until he was taken out by US forces in June 2006. He created an embryonic form of IS and some of his more educated associates set up a plan that was to run from 9/11 to the foundation of a caliphate in Syria between 2013 and 2016.[4] The Zarqawi plan was either very prescient or IS leaders were following his script. The plan promised massive campaigns of international terrorism after the caliphate was established and then 'final victory' of worldwide Islamism by 2020. Most of the dystopian future envisaged was based upon the importance of a territorial state, not least to entice worldwide volunteers. Perhaps 30,000 heeded the call (out of 1.6 billion Muslims who were supposed to obey the new caliph). Even at the height of its power, by any normal measure it was a failed state. Jihadists, however, would argue that their governance was very good considering the most powerful countries in the world were bombing the hell out of an infant landlocked state that had almost zero air defence. Adherents of the master plan assumed that al-Qaeda and IS would reunify – that could happen when IS loses all its territory and reverts to an underground organisation which it was under the US occupation of Iraq. The plan also prophesied that the US economy would collapse and that a spectacular attack would be launched on Israel. Osama bin Laden disavowed the plan before he was killed but many IS leaders still believe in its eventual fulfilment not least as part of the end times prophecies. So what next?

> In a nutshell, the current incarnation of the Islamic State emerged from the remnant of the Islamic State of Iraq, which was devastated by the Awakening and the Surge from 2007-2010. But it was not defeated and it regenerated stronger than it had been previously. The United States and the rest of the Islamic State's enemies are in the process of 'defeating' the jihadi group once again. The big long-term question is whether they will finish the job this time and, if not, how strong the Islamic State will be when it regenerates.[5]

Even if IS mends fences with al-Qaeda and other local Islamist militias they are unlikely to attract a mass following from the majority in the *Umma*. IS regards many of the world's Muslims as apostates worthy of death and so most Muslims will shun IS. Al-Qaeda's image has softened because of inevitable comparison with IS, though its followers are hardly treehugging vegans. Al-Qaeda has probably killed more Muslims than anybody else. The vast majority of Muslims are running away from both jihadist groups. The jihadists will continue to kill many people but the dream of a globe-spanning caliphate grows ever more distant. 'Final victory' looks very unlikely in the foreseeable future. It is an Islamic La La Land. *Inshallah.*

After IS

If IS jihadists travel to Libya to join the core reserve caliphate they have tried to set up there, then North Africa could be in for a torrid time. Even apart from IS mischief-making the Maghreb has lots of its own time-bombs waiting to blow. Each country is dysfunctional in its own way. Algeria, for example, has gone quiet recently but when its long-term and ailing 80-year-old dictator, Abdelaziz Bouteflika, dies, the country may well implode. The Islamists, who have been suppressed by his iron fist, will fill the political vacuum. The tensions that have been buried since the long and bloody civil war will re-emerge. Europe, especially the former metropole, France, could be swamped by literally millions of refugees. This could dwarf the refugee drama caused by Syria. IS Mark 2, enveloping Libya, Algeria and Tunisia – just across the Med from Europe – would be a security nightmare.

Daniel Greenfield, a Shillman Journalism Fellow at the Freedom Centre, is a New York-based writer who has specialised in radical Islam. He predicted that there would be a permanent refugee problem in the Middle East even without the Syrian civil war.[6] And even without the Sunni-Shia Cold War the refugees would still be coming. The vast majority of civil wars over the last ten years have broken out in Muslim countries, he said. Many of these countries are also poor and have very high birth rates. Greenfield summarises the problem: 'Combine violence and poverty with a population boom and you get a permanent migration crisis.'

He has a point because the Muslim world is expanding beyond the means to sustain itself. Greenfield, who is an Israeli, argued that, in both the Middle East and Asia, Muslims underperform in comparison with their non-Muslim neighbours, especially in education and business. Historically, oil was the only asset that boosted the weak Arab economies and now in the age of fracking and electric cars that is a diminishing asset. Muslim societies, with much lower literacy rates, especially for women, are never going to compete with modern economies. Nor will unstable dictatorships provide stopgaps for their anaemic polities, except subsidised bread and perhaps circuses. The Arab Spring was largely a Western delusion – reform has not got anywhere in the Arab world except to kick-start primitive Islamism. Rewinding the clock back to the seventh century is inevitably going to make it harder to keep up with modernity. Expanding populations, divided along ethnic, tribal or religious lines, are competing over power, wealth and land (much of it desert).

Greenfield asserts that only two solutions exist: war or migration.

Even if the West had not invaded Iraq the basic problems would still be much the same as today. Baghdad has one of the highest densities in the world. Greenfield argues – wrongly I believe – that Muslim societies such as Iraq or Afghanistan *want* Western interventions so as to inject money/aid into their bankrupt states. So violence is a sort of economic blackmail. The only alternative, in Greenfield's analysis, is to emigrate. For thousands of dollars, a would-be refugee can pay to be smuggled into Europe. It's a relatively small investment with a big pay off. Even the lowest state benefits in Sweden or England are higher than the average wage at home. That is why Muslims tend to travel to cities in richer countries with advanced welfare systems such as Germany. Personally I think people risking so much to cross into Europe are keener on a new life via a job, not to scrounge benefits. Greenfield is correct, however, in saying that the journey is an investment for an entire extended family; once the young man gets his papers, the family reunification begins. Human trafficking doesn't just involve rafts and leaky boats; in Muslim societies it is more about family connections. *Connections* are the way of doing any serious business in the Arab world. If it's not family sponsorship then it can involve crime syndicates: many of the technically unemployed in Western Europe make black money from slave labour, prostitution and drugs.

Not all the migrants are Muslim of course. Many of the recent arrivals in Italy come from West Africa, from Christian as well as Islamic backgrounds. They pay around 1,500 euros to cross the Med. Actually they pay to travel to the twelve-mile territorial limit of Libya's waters where they are picked up, often by prior arrangement, by NGO rescue boats. The EU border agency, Frontex, has accused some of the NGOs of complicity with the people smugglers. If the Western fleets did not patrol there would be far fewer deaths because far fewer migrants and smugglers would set sail to cross the whole Med, especially in winter. Bombing the smuggling boats in their ports was not altogether a bad idea – it would have saved tens of thousands of lives.

Turkey, an increasingly Islamist society built on a pile of debt, once wanted to join the EU. And the EU pretended it *could* join one day. Turkey was held up as a modern Muslim society that could bridge East and West.

Recep Tayyip Erdogan, the Turkish president, recently persuaded the EU to grant visa-free travel for his 75 million people, in exchange for controlling the refugee exodus from Syria. After the modernisers closed the caliphate in 1924 Turkey gradually developed a secular democracy, occasionally suffering, or enjoying, military coups to enforce secularism as advocated by the founder of the state, Kemal Atatürk. The tragedy is that Erdogan has taken the country back to religious dictatorship. The president is a clever and patient Islamist who famously compared democracy to a bus ride; when it gets him to where he wants to travel, he will get off. The Turkish strongman has even commissioned a new golden throne to sit on. Turning his back on Western liberal democracy he has talked of reviving regional influence as in the days of the Sublime Porte, the Ottoman empire. The would-be Istanbul caliph has consolidated power around himself by taking it away from the military, the judiciary and the media and stifling nearly all domestic dissent – although what he calls 'Mountain Turks' (Kurds) remain a large and increasingly hostile minority.

You could argue that Western interventions in the Muslim world, no matter how misguided, are attempts to manage basic Islamic dysfunction in government. The idea that the West intervened to steal the oil is nonsense. It is much cheaper just to buy it rather than spend trillions on invading Iraq or liberating Kuwait. The West did not invent Arab dysfunction, though sometimes it made it worse. And yet the West – even when it provides massive humanitarian support such as feeding refugees from Syria in camps in adjacent counties – keeps on taking the blame for self-made Arab dysfunction. The refugee crisis is a structural problem independent of Western actions. And as Chancellor Merkel discovered, the flood of refugees can be infinite. Even if the civil wars end, millions will still want to leave as economic refugees.

It is no surprise that terrorism and crime are increasingly caused by Muslim immigrants. If Muslims cannot reconcile their problems at home, why should they suddenly be capable of reconciling them in Europe? They are exporting their problems – by the millions. As Greenfield succinctly says:

Distance is no answer. Travel is no cure …. We can't save Muslims from themselves. We can only save ourselves from their violence. The permanent Muslim refugee crisis will never stop being our crisis unless we close the door.

Greenfield has offered a typical hardline Israeli viewpoint. He is articulate but he overstates his case. For common humanity we should still try to ease conditions, and where possible help to seek a ceasefire and ideally some interim settlement, for example, in Syria. Helping provide housing and, above all, factories to employ Jordanians in tandem with local Syrian refugees is one very partial answer. Money should be spent in the region to help the displaced in situ, not in Europe. And some genuinely unaccompanied young children or seriously wounded should be taken to Europe from the camps in Jordan or Lebanon, not least to stop money being poured into the big crime networks and human traffickers.

Migration or war may not be the only solutions. Other alternatives may exist. Firstly, let's take a somewhat fluffy alternative. The most republican country on earth, the USA, often seems to hanker after monarchy. The Americans loved Princess Diana, for example. After the Americans took over, nobody asked the Iraqis if they preferred the return of a king rather than another corrupt commoner. The Americans have never got over booting out King George III. Yet some surviving loyalists in the US and Canada ask whether the 240-year experiment in rebellion against the British Crown has worked, especially after the election of Trump. If Queen Elizabeth II is good enough for the Canadians, or the ever-truculent Aussies, then why not a US return to the Crown as well? They could do, and perhaps now have, done worse. The American government would have to apologise to Queen Elizabeth II, but no compensation would be demanded.

In Libya, after the fall of Gaddafi, why was the massive display of royalist flags ignored? In Afghanistan, the charming old king, Zahir Shah, was persuaded to rule himself out when the Americans were hunting around to replace the Taliban. Look at the old newsreels of the 1960s when the king led the country – women were not wearing veils, they were pictured attending university in shortish skirts. Admittedly they were usually filmed in Kabul, yet it looks light years away from the Islamist days of the Taliban or even today. It is true that King Farouk of Egypt was too much of a playboy to do much for his subjects but he was reputedly good natured and friendly towards some of his Jewish and Christian minorities. The Saudi royals are corrupt, xenophobic and dangerous advocates of firebrand Wahhabism and the West supports them, misguidedly. And yet, at the other royal extreme, the West rubs along fine with the Jordanian and Moroccan monarchies and a few other constitutional royals. They are perhaps reassuring beacons in the region.

Encouraging constitutional monarchy is a cosmetic sticking plaster, not an answer to the deep-rooted malaise of poor Arab governance. Two of the main structural problems of the Middle East are how leaders are made and, secondly, the actual shape of the countries these bad rulers try to lead. The question was not resolved even by the Prophet – disputes about who should be *khalifa*, successors, were eventually embroiled in tribal and personal rivalries that partly account for today's Shi'a versus Sunni chasm. When Turkish, Mongol or even Persian converts ran the Islamic show, the caliphs still were paranoid. The Ottomans conscripted Christians to help run their vast empire and, on securing the throne, the caliphs made sure their own blood brothers were ritually strangled with a silk cord to forestall rival claims. Even when colonialism was overcome – the notion of republican democracy, especially Arab socialism, was a mere mask for dictatorship, as Nasser proved. One of the factors that prompted the widespread Arab revolts in 2011 was hostility to hereditary succession. Dictators in Egypt and Libya particularly were trying to finesse dynasties by grooming their sons to follow them as Hafez al-Assad had already done in Syria. In the end the only thing that was democratised was violence. Everybody fought everyone else in the living nightmare of the Syrian civil war.

If Arab leaders have usually failed their people since the death of the Prophet, and especially since the end of the Great War, what is the fundamental answer?

A root and branch reform could be redrawing the map of the Middle East. The very name 'Middle East' must demand an answer to 'east of where?' It is based on a European view of the world, of course. And it is Europeans who shaped the countries. They drew boundary lines that did not exist before and created crazily artificial borders sometimes, just as they did in Africa. Arabs (and Africans) are now trying to redraw these borders in their own blood. Maybe the West should help them – redraw lines, that is, not in their own blood, although most leaders are rather reluctant to spill their own blood.

Hardly anybody is content with their current borders. The Islamic State's essential mission was to annihilate the century-old Sykes-Picot borders. That's why one of their first propaganda videos was to film a bulldozer breaking through a sand berm that constituted part of the Iraq-Syria border. To the north of IS are the Kurds, the most betrayed people in recent history; the biggest minority in the world without their own country. Some of the Sunnis in Iraq and Syria tended to tolerate IS because they hated the Shi'ite rulers in Baghdad and the Alawite dictator in Damascus far more. The Iranians do not want Sunni power to be revived, especially in Iraq, partly because of the savage eight-year war with Saddam. Israel has always disputed its borders but it's pleased to see Hezbollah fighting fellow Arabs in Syria. That state – Israel's most potent foe historically – has essentially collapsed into a military maelstrom. Iran is mired in endless wars to its west and in the south, in Yemen, fighting with Saudi Arabia. IS has never deployed its best propaganda weapon – a diversionary attack, through the Golan, on Israel. And for Jerusalem, that Israel's enemies are busy with so much in-fighting means that everyone else has forgotten the Palestinian cause.

Are there no long-term solutions?

Syria's unravelling has set a possible example for a large-scale re-alignment. Suggesting redrawing maps can be a messy business, even for writers as well as statesmen. I wrote a chapter in a book published by Oxford University Press in 1977 in which I suggested a 'whitestan' in apartheid South Africa's Cape Province.[7] It was rather tongue-in-cheek indicating that the whites should control a territory proportionate to their population size, to avoid endless war. A nuclear-armed garrison state, with its white and mixed-race Afrikaans-speaking population, would have a large majority over indigenous black Africans, in that province, the original home of the Dutch colony. It caused a fuss and yet I am surprised to see that there is today a movement to set up an independent Cape province, an area which is already run by the main opposition party, because of the inept kleptocracy that is the African National Congress government in Pretoria. More recently I wrote a series of articles about truncating Pakistan to re-unite the Pathans with their brothers in Afghanistan.[8] That caused a few media barbs – in the days before social media trolling. I am not the only aspiring radical political cartographer working on this region, however. In June 2006 Lieutenant Colonel Ralph Peters published a powerfully argued new map for the Middle East in the *Armed Forces Journal*.[9] This was dubbed the 'blood borders' map. In September 2013 a former journalist colleague from my African days, Robin Wright, wrote a lively piece in the *New York Times,* partly based on the blood borders map but also developing the argument for the re-division of Libya.[10]

Peters listed a long series of 'colossal, manmade deformities that will not stop generating hatred and violence'. He made the frequently addressed – but never resolved – complaint that over 35 million Kurds do not have their own homeland. Peters wrote his paper in 2006 and already the Kurds in Iraq have their own de facto state, and probably – not least after giving so much military help to the US Army – the Kurds of Syria, or some of them, might get to join a bigger Free Kurdistan. Prising free the millions of oppressed Kurds in Turkey and Iran will not be easy but such an entity would be the 'most pro-Western state between Bulgaria and Japan', said Peters. He also delineated a Shia state in southern Iraq, thus leaving a Sunni state in the north-west to join their Sunni brothers in Syria. Peters argued that the Saudi state 'is the worst thing to happen to Muslims since the days of the Prophet … and the worst thing to happen to Arabs since the Ottoman (if not the Mongol) conquest'. For a retired US colonel, he was not pulling his punches. Personally, I would agree. Peters advocated a sort of super-Vatican for the cities of Mecca and Medina, administered by a council of the representatives of the world's major Muslim schools. No doubt that would be a recipe for endless (but perhaps bloodless) argument. The Saudi oilfields would go to a Shia sub-region, while a south-eastern quadrant would be allocated to Yemen. Confined to a rump state around Riyadh, the House of Saud would then be capable of far less international mischief. Iran should not gloat. In an ideal world, its madcap boundaries would be redrawn to create a unified Azerbaijan, Free Kurdistan, the Arab Shia state and Free Baluchistan. It would regain the province of Herat in Afghanistan, and thus become a Persian state once more. Afghanistan would regain its tribal territories from Pakistan and unite the Pathan peoples on both sides of the colonially demarcated border. Pakistan, like Saudi Arabia, is not a natural organic state. In its third partition it would say goodbye to its vast southern territory to a Free Baluchistan. The city states of the UAE would be incorporated into a large Shia state ringing much of the Persian Gulf. Peters reduced Israel's borders to the pre-1967 ones, which would make it indefensible. That wouldn't work and Washington would never allow it. Peters also imagined a greater Jordan, at the Saudis' expense, which would have made T.E. Lawrence smile.

Much of the rest is, of course, equally fanciful but it makes the point that so many existing borders are unnatural and dangerous. The IS had a point in making their first actions as a state an attack on Sykes-Picot. It is clear that today's unjust and unstable borders in the region, to borrow from Churchill, generate more trouble than can be consumed locally.

Robin Wright's piece in the *New York Times* was written in 2013, two years after the recent upheavals on the Arab streets. She suggested an Alawite homeland which the 2017 battlefields are shaping in that direction anyway. Her article is interesting on Libya which she divided into three: the two historic Roman parts would become independent as Tripolitania and Cyrenaica, with a third Fezzan state in the southern deserts. Fezzan is more Sahelian than North African in culture and tribal identity. Wright divides Yemen into north and south again, the two states of just a few decades ago. She is also tough on Saudi Arabia and breaks it up into the five regions that preceded the modern state. Wright also suggested the recognition of city states including well-armed enclaves such as Misurata in Libya or a capital with multiple identities such as Baghdad. Homogenous zones like Jabal al-Druze in southern Syria could make an autonomous comeback as well.

Let's look at three of these proposals in a little more depth. First, the Saudis. Despite adopting much of the Saudis' Wahhabi theology and its use of Saudi schoolbooks, volunteer fighters, imams and lawyers, the Islamic State has always loathed Saudi Arabia, despite all the money that came from the Riyadh government and individual donors. Part of the reason is the IS view that the royal family is a blasphemy against the rule of Allah. One part of the apocalypse that the end times will bring is an uprising against the House of Saud; this in turn would wreck the Western economies. It would also, inter alia, collapse Jordan, a Saudi client state and Western ally. Islamists would inherit these states, the jihadists believe, and thus put them in position to liberate Jerusalem. This sounds so farfetched but predicting a large caliphate in 2013 would have been laughed at too.

The standard Western response is that no matter how medieval, indolent and corrupt the Saudis are, they are better than a jihadist state, the almost inevitable outcome of a royal collapse. Also, defenders of the Saudi royals point out that they are generally more liberal and certainly more pro-Western than the general population. It is argued that the desert kingdom, which lucked out on oil deposits rather than making anything, is about to face serious upheavals domestically, not least because of the precipitous fall in oil prices. Already the mollycoddled Saudi citizens are seeing their enormous benefits cut back. The House of Saud has survived only because it could buy off so many of its own citizens. The West should start preparing for a new dispensation in the kingdom and maybe start reducing its massive arms sales and training. Wahhabism, the one thing that seems to bloom in the desert, is likely to blossom even more. Born in the eighteenth century in a desert and from a sacred book and at a time of tribal massacres, it developed into an ultra fundamentalist sect with a surreal relationship with women, ferocious religious laws and a xenophobic hostility to outsiders, including many Muslims. Saudi Arabia is a *Daesh*, an IS, that made it. As Kamel Daoud, the well-known Algerian novelist and newspaper columnist for *Quotidien d'Oran*, noted:

> The West's denial regarding Saudi Arabia is striking: it salutes the theocracy as its ally but pretends not to notice that it is the world's chief ideological sponsor of Islamist culture. The younger generations of radicals in the so-called Arab world were not born jihadists. They were suckled in the bosom of Fatwa Valley, a kind of Islamist Vatican with a vast industry that produces theologians, religious laws, books and aggressive editorial policies and media campaigns ... .
>
> *Daesh* [IS] has a mother: the invasion of Iraq. But it also has a father: Saudi Arabia and its religious-industrial complex. Until that point is understood, battles may be won but the war will be lost. Jihadists will be killed, only to be reborn in future generations and raised on the same books.

The Saudi media campaigns have been picked up by other Arabic-language TV stations that pump out the Islamist vision. These are often taken up by numerous Islamic stations in other languages. Take Urdu as one example; many Muslim households in the UK look at and believe satellite Urdu channels. They are often very sceptical about the BBC. If only the West could read the Arabic of many Islamist newspapers. The West is portrayed as a depraved land of pornographic, drunken whore-mongering infidels. The attacks in Brussels and Paris are portrayed as the results of the Western onslaught on the *Umma*. Jews are castigated. Iraq and Palestine are constantly regurgitated along with the colonial traumas; and all this is couched in a Koranic messianic context. The leaders of these Islamic countries, especially Saudi Arabia, will send condolences to Paris or Brussels and denounce the crimes against humanity. This is as schizophrenic as the West's profession of friendship towards the chief jihadist enemy, Saudi Arabia.

Thus Saudi Arabia is the main jihadist problem for the West. The Saudis have spent billions and billions spreading their crazed brand of Islam. The Saudis were ultimately behind the deaths of many Western troops in Afghanistan – by supporting Pakistani extremists. Pakistan and its financial backer Saudi Arabia have been our enemy in Afghanistan, not the Taliban (who were also created by Pakistan with Saudi money). Even moderate states such as the Maldives are being poisoned by Saudi money and religious extremists. They are trying to buy an atoll or two for a private royal pleasure park. In public the Saudi elite are ultra religious – in private often boozy hedonists. And yet they pretend formal piety, paying for mosques, religious schools and extremist propaganda across the planet.

In the UK the Saudis have also corrupted politics, most famously by blackmailing Blair's Labour government into stopping the Serious Fraud Office from investigating massive corruption in British arms sales. The biggest deal was done by the Tories, however, negotiated by Margaret Thatcher and her wayward son. Maybe we should just stop selling weapons to this ultra-dangerous state with an abominable human rights record, both at home and in their war in next-door Yemen. It could be argued that more people have been beheaded in Saudi Arabia than in its offspring, the Islamic State.

The redrawing of Saudi Arabia's very recent and very artificial borders would make a lot of sense. The Hashemites in Jordan had a better claim, as Lawrence of Arabia argued. So many Shias who are oppressed in the country might also be happy. It could be maintained that even the Turks would do a better job of running an Islamic version of the Vatican states, incorporating Mecca and Medina. After all, they ran the holy sites for many hundreds of years. Anybody would be more ecumenical than the Saudis have been.

Pakistan is an even more dangerous state than their Saudi friend, not least because of the so-called 'loose nukes'. The Saudis paid for some of the approximately 350 nuclear warheads that Pakistan owns. Riyadh reckons they are a useful insurance if Iran gets too nuclear and too confrontational. The Saudis would just ask for some of the warheads they have invested so much in. Some of these warheads are thought to be low-yield tactical weapons. Tactical is a misnomer because *any* use of nukes crosses the biggest red line possible. Even Barack Obama would agree. The Pakistanis have been responsible for endless terrorism in the UK, ceaseless meddling in wars in Afghanistan and Kashmir as well as terrorist attacks on its big neighbour, India. Allegedly, India has adopted a strategy called 'Cold Start'. In short India has enough battlegroups on standby to surge into Pakistan on several fronts and thus seize enough Pakistani territory to bargain with, and therefore avoid a nuclear confrontation between the two inheritors of the Raj. They have fought a series of nasty wars since the catastrophic bloodshed of partition in 1947-48. Pakistanis argued privately that they have to deploy tac-nukes in a ready state to stop the Cold Start surge. The increasingly religiously extremist country suffers from many Islamist rogue elements in its own forces, including the all-powerful ISI intelligence service. America, which once helped guard the nukes, knows that the command and control procedures for these tactical and strategic weapons are vulnerable. In the last five years terrorists have attacked a number of facilities that house the nukes. For example, the Kamra air force base near Islamabad has been attacked three times by Islamists belonging to the Tehreek-i-Taliban Pakistan.

The bankrupt economy, the constant destabilisation from the tribal areas between Pakistan and Afghanistan, the endemic distrust between civilian politicians and the armed forces, the numerous jihadist groups inside Pakistan, some run and paid by the ISI, all add up to the most threatening nuclear crisis in the world. The North Korean leadership runs a highly disciplined and controlled country that is nowhere near as dangerous as the chaotic potential for rogue attacks in Pakistan. Another partition in the Islamic country would do much for international security. Free Baluchistan and an enlarged Afghanistan would make many millions of locals very happy. Kashmir should be united, possibly under UN or Indian control. Before a much smaller central Pakistan emerges, the existing country has to be defanged of its nukes. Technically the Americans could do this physically and with cyber power, which is one reason why Pakistani leaders are rightly paranoid. The rump de-nuclearised Pakistan could become another angry Gaza but next-door India's power would be so enhanced that its highly professional forces could keep the peace.

Professor Richard Hass, president of America's non-partisan Council on Foreign Relations, is one of the wisest and most respected experts on international relations. He explained why Pakistan is probably the most dangerous country in the world: 'toxic mix of nuclear weapons, terrorists, weak civilian authority and limited governmental capacity, and the intensity of its animosity toward India'.

Reshaping the recent artificial states of Pakistan and Saudi Arabia could do the world a very big favour – for Muslims and non-believers alike. Such radical surgery may be the only way of destroying the roots and the culture of jihadism. It would be the understatement of the century to say that Pakistan's and Saudi Arabia's governments would not be keen to accept their own dismemberment. Pakistan, though, is a completely failed state propped up by money from Saudi Arabia and Washington. And the Saudi economy could collapse in the near future. In short, Saudi resistance will be weakened by the lack of wherewithal to resist. Moreover, perhaps the majority of Sunni Muslims would prefer the removal of Wahhabism and jihadism in both countries. The hundreds of millions of Shia would surely agree, especially if a new dispensation could allow ease of *haj* access to the holy cities in Arabia. The creation of a new cartological architecture in both states is more likely than the IS caliphate seemed only four years ago. Events are moving very fast in the febrile Islamic world. And surely it is better to try to change borders by diplomatic persuasion and economic pressures rather than the barbaric slaughter of the IS approach to redrawing boundaries.

Meanwhile, let's look at building a brand new organic state rather than the partitions of two unnatural ones. Free Kurdistan has a nice ring to it, after the century of injustices Kurds have suffered at the hands of the Versailles peacemakers and local tyrants, most notably Saddam Hussein. Today the Kurds are on the threshold of achieving their dreams: by fighting for them. Peshmerga volunteers from Iraqi Kurdistan usually work in shifts, spending up to ten days at a time on the front line and twenty days away from it. They get paid erratically. Many have to borrow money to fight. They usually lack proper uniforms, decent boots, binoculars and night-vision goggles, let alone modern weapons. This is largely a civilian army who have to hold down jobs and feed their families. They do it out of a sense of duty and to free their land. Many older fighters remember the massacres by the Iraqi government, especially the 1988 gassing of thousands at Halabja. Their own history of persecution means that they have sheltered two million refugees from minority communities such as the Yazidis and Christians; plus they are looking after many Sunni Arabs. And yet with the drop in the price of oil and lack of financial support from Baghdad they are trying to help these millions without proper resources. The refugee numbers are likely to swell once Mosul finally falls.

The Kurds in Syria and Iraq have fought IS to protect their traditional homeland. They also realise that their traditional foes, the Arabs, are more likely to leave them alone if the Arabs fight among themselves. The IS threatened the Kurdish heartlands and made big inroads into their territory but paradoxically it's the presence of IS which stops Baghdad consolidating its central power and challenging the notion of Kurdish independence. So what happens when Raqqa and Mosul fall and IS as a state is defeated? The Americans may feel grateful now to their proxy Kurdish forces but in the future will they recognise Kurdistan? Will Washington return the military favour by stepping in to stop Iraq or Turkey crushing the Kurds?

Kurds have a very long history of being shafted once their temporary military usefulness is surplus to requirements. Perhaps the greatest warrior in Islamic history was Saladin, a Kurd. Ever since then their role as fighters and mercenaries has been recognised. In the late Ottoman period the sultan formed a deadly Kurdish cavalry unit. Kemal Atatürk promised the Kurds autonomy for their support of his revolutionary movement but, when he won, the promise to the Kurds was forgotten. More recently Ankara has tried to divide and rule by establishing Kurdish militias and home guards in the Kurdish-dominated areas of the east. Despite the good weapons and pay for these militias, the internal Turkish Kurdish opposition, the PKK, is still the dominant force among Kurds. In the past Baghdad also set up various militias to divide and rule in their Kurdish majority areas. At other times Baghdad simply indulged in ethnic cleansing. The Iranian government supported the two main Kurdish parties in Iraq (KDP and PUK) to undermine Baghdad, while in turn Iraq gave aid to Iranian Kurdish parties. The Syrian government in Damascus also backed the Iraqi Kurds to weaken their Ba'athist rivals in Baghdad; and the elder Assad granted asylum and bases to the PKK. From 1972 to 1975 Iran, Israel and Washington had a tripartite agreement to destabilise the Ba'athist regime in Baghdad by arming the Kurds. Confusing? Well, this is the simplified version of how Kurds have been manipulated and it worked because they are also a very quarrelsome people.

Kurds have had a long relationship with Washington. American airpower helped them after the first US-led war against Saddam by eventually creating a safe haven in the north. The Kurds also helped US forces in the northern front in the 2003 war against Saddam. In the current war against IS, the Americans have provided money, weapons, special forces and air support along the 1,000-kilometre front. The Kurds in Syria have a much shorter relationship with the US but they have fought so well that they have become recognised proxies. The Syrian PYD (and its militias, mainly YPG) are an offshoot of the PKK – its Marxist-Leninist policies do not make the Americans happy. Washington pretends that the Syrian Kurds are *not* an offshoot of their Turkish PKK parents and have no relations at all, so as to prevent a rupture with Turkey. Ankara has blamed Assad for the murderous chaos in the region and that is why it initially backed IS before the jihadists turned on their most strategically important ally. Ankara regarded PYD and its military wings as mortal enemies because they were seen as the vanguard for a big PKK insurrection within Turkey itself. Washington was thus forced to turn a Nelsonian eye to Turkish air force attacks on PKK Kurds in Turkey and Iraq. Then Russia intervened and YPG were courted by both Moscow and Washington as formidable fighters against IS. The only alternative was for Turkey to take the main brunt of the war against its one-time allies, IS, which Ankara was very reluctant to do, especially with domestic terrorism and political instability raging at home.

The Kurds know that allies have always been fickle but without US airpower Erbil and Kobani would have been lost to IS at the start of the fighting in 2014. All the major powers, especially America, are theoretically committed to preserving the integrity of Iraq and Syria, let alone Turkey. The Kurds have to unite among themselves – a big ask, bearing in mind the centuries of divide and conquer by their neighbours. They have to show they can unite and administer their own areas properly. They have shown they can fight but can they govern? Would a Free Kurdistan, initially including Syrian and Iraqi Kurds, work, for the Kurds and the region?

Kurds are usually seen as plucky underdogs who fight bravely with poor weapons. That is true. But Kurds are also their own worst enemies. The Kurds' recent ethnic cleansing of their own has brought little media attention. It is also true that Saddam drove out Kurds and paid for Arabs to take over previous Kurdish areas, especially in the oil-rich north. That is why so many Arabs sympathised with IS. Now the Kurds are taking back their former areas and are said to be demolishing Arab homes. The West went to war over ethnic cleansing in Bosnia and Kosovo; now its allies are doing it, though arguably on a much smaller scale. And the multi-racial nature of Iraqi Kurdistan is obvious with the acceptance of so many Arab and other refugees. Another criticism of the Kurds is their chronic tribal disunity which is partly represented in the two main parties, the KDP and PUK. Even the Peshmerga fighting force is effectively run by two parties; when they fight alongside each other against IS everyone knows who is PUK and who is KDP. They have bashed each other, especially in the 1990s. More recently a third-force Kurdish political party has tried to end the old dichotomy.

Iraqi Kurdistan is also broke because of the double whammy of millions of refugees and low oil prices. It also doesn't help that Baghdad doesn't pay government workers, including army and police. And like nearly all oil economies, corruption is a major destabilising force. The

Syrian YPG has lots of skeletons in its cupboard too, not least its tactical alliance with Damascus. This has incited proxy wars not just between the Pentagon and the CIA but also USA versus its NATO ally Turkey. The Syrian Kurds have different tribal alliances from the Iraqi Kurds and especially dislike President Masoud Barzani of the autonomous Iraqi region. Because the PKK is a banned terrorist organisation in the UK and USA, the West has had to pretend the PKK and YPG are entirely different. This is a fiction to match the similar Western diplomatic fiction that Syria and Iraq must remain unitary states. This takes us back to the problem of unnatural states. Believing in Iraq is like a Muslim believing in the Holy Trinity: three cannot be one.

Conclusion

We can work it out

I have tried to be optimistic in his book, albeit not, I hope, mindlessly so. People moan about Brexit but it could have been worse: Jeremy Corbyn could have become prime minister. Likewise, imagine Sarah Palin in the White House; that puts Trump in a better perspective, maybe. If the CIA knows its stuff, it would have put dud codes in the so-called atomic football. If Hillary had got in, she would have no doubt been saner, but her hawkishness might have exacerbated the already bad relations with Russia. Before the apparently Putin-friendly new American administration, relations with Moscow were poised between a new Cold War and the start of a Third World War. Whether Trump's big *volte face* over Syria throws détente with Russia back into the ice age is a moot point. It might have just been a case of temporary missile envy.

As ever the Islamic world is out of the step with the rest of the planet's progress, not least in developing more ideological – Islamist – paradigms. Elsewhere the old models are disappearing and introducing instead, for example, China's brand of post-communist Confucianism and a Russian Eastern-Orthodox sense of national identity. The *ideological* zero-sum clashes of the once and future superpowers – USA, Russia and China – are in decline if not over. The disputes are now about traditional great-power realpolitik. Machiavelli has replaced Marx, thank goodness. My god died in Auschwitz and now I am waiting for the religious bigots, including Muslims, Christians or Jews, to catch up with Darwin. I love the true story of when a senior cleric in Saudi Arabia was told to wind in his neck. He had banged on about the earth-shattering impact of women ever being permitted to drive in the kingdom, but he overreached himself when he preached a fatwa against anyone suggesting the earth was round. A minor

Saudi prince had actually been up in the space station. This was a big deal for the Saudis and naturally the prince described the beauty, and *shape*, of the earth, which got the imam going again till the religious police knocked on his door.

Who would have thought religion would become a prime mover in international relations again? Who would have thought it possible that a revival of the caliphate, ninety years after it was closed down in Istanbul, would phoenix and shake the globe? Religion aside, the international system is being questioned like never before. China is challenging in the South China Sea and Russia in Ukraine to take but two prominent examples. The traditional Westphalian rules invented by the Europeans are everywhere in tatters. Certainly the old European clubs, especially the European Union, and perhaps NATO, are being shaken roughly by their well-tailored collars, just as many countries have quit the International Criminal Court for being a white man's club for ex-colonials.

Nevertheless, in the post-ideological world, outside Islam, deals can be done, and not just by the man who sees himself as the best dealmaker in the world, Donald Trump. If they can finesse their immediate differences over the US cruise missile strikes, the new American president could work with Putin to fix a settlement in Syria after they co-operate to finish off the Islamic State. Beijing should be consulted because it too has concerns about Islamist threats, including (exaggerated and self-serving) fears of jihadism inside China. If the ultra-complex problems of Syria can be resolved by the great powers, then Ukraine should be more straightforward, provided NATO is strengthened and the Baltic states reassured – the old big stick and soft words again. Washington could also work with Beijing on the sensitive politics of Taiwan. Again, Trump's boost to the US Navy allows America to deal with China's local bullying from a position of strength. Washington appeared to believe that democracy was in retreat under Obama. Now that may be changing, for the better.

A strong foreign policy cannot be sustained without a strong domestic economy, however. The US debt is now $14 trillion, roughly 75 per cent of GDP. In a decade it could be 80 or 90 per cent. No country, not even a superpower, can maintain that level of debt, without major growth in the domestic economy. The debt is also potentially vulnerable to manipulation if China *in extremis* decides to dump its dollars. That would be self-mutilating, except if Beijing felt its crucial interests, perhaps the security and status of Taiwan, were seriously threatened.

Russia has been accused of many things recently; certainly Putin has not been sitting on his hands. He is alleged to have encouraged Russian donors to bankroll Marine Le Pen in France. I am writing this before the 2017 French general election but in the unlikely event she wins then it would mean, according to Niall Ferguson's recent argument in the UK *Sunday Times,*

> that all five permanent members of the UN security council would ultimately all be either populist or authoritarian-controlled …. Thus might the institutions of collective security be serving the interests of the great powers as never before: the ultimate revenge of realpolitik.

I am not sure I fully agree that Theresa May's Tories fit into this description although the June 2017 election was predicted to create a landslide victory that could have forged a right-wing triumphalism in the Conservative party. It didn't happen. And France's Front National's victory is possible, in 2022, but still as unlikely as Brexit. The diplomatic coalition of yesteryear – USA, China, Russia, France and Britain – might seem implausible but it was this coalition that won the Second World War and it would be ironic if a similar line-up prevented a Third World War. To get the five permanent members of the Security Council to join the same chorus and sing in tune seems a harmony too far perhaps.

Nor does this scenario include the political chaos caused by Islamism. I have made many suggestions in this book, ranging from military containment to exhortations to reform. The cancer of Islamism is essentially a problem of Islam, for Muslims to cure or excise. Unfortunately, even if Islamic regimes have enough groundswell of popular support to risk dramatic religious reforms, they probably won't have the time. It is also (highly) unlikely that some of my major suggestions, such as dismembering Saudi Arabia, which is masquerading as a normal Westphalian state, and denuding Pakistan of its nukes, will be enacted. Immediate harsh surgery, starting with the kinetic finale of the Islamic State, will be required, however. Islamism in Europe is a virus parasitic on Western liberalism; its tolerant philosophy allows it a place to flourish. For example, there is a tacit alliance between liberals and extremists on the veil. The whole purpose of al-Qaeda's attacks on the West, starting with the Twin Towers, was to force an authoritarian response, with the West invading the Middle East, so as to polarise the rift between Muslims and unbelievers. This has happened to some extent in Europe where most counterterrorism measures, for example Prevent in Britain, are regarded by most Muslims as spying and snooping. If the Islamist attacks continue, as they are likely to after the collapse of the Islamic State, then the liberal democracies in Europe may self-mutilate their own ideals and become far less liberal, in order to survive. In this respect Islamist extremists will have won.

European cultures are changing and not always for the good. Some liberal commentators treat the new populism as a political illness, a xenophobic regression. One of the best analyses of this debate is David Goodheart's recent book, *The Road to Somewhere: The Populist Revolt and the Future of Politics*. He divides Brits into more universal, wealthier, better educated types who are citizens of 'everywhere', at least everywhere in Europe. The second group, the 'somewheres', are more committed to their historical background, home area and patriotism. I have simplified here because Goodheart does *not* make Brexiteers look like rednecks with hangovers and chainsaws, *Deliverance* without the banjos. He mentions Gus O'Donnell, the former cabinet secretary. In my time in Whitehall he was nicknamed after his initials, GOD, and he was indeed very powerful. Goodheart quotes him as a standard-bearer for supranationalism when he said that he saw his responsibility as 'to maximise global welfare not national welfare'. Such an attitude did not wash with the majority of Brits, who were tired of experts and elitism. It was not just a question of putting the British tribe first. Yes, that was important: control of immigration and reforms such as national identity cards were allied with beliefs in rewarding effort and contribution to society, and not just financial ones. The majority of people in the UK felt that their political leaders were no longer listening. The reasons were many – from the expenses scandals in parliament to gross inequality in taxation and not keeping promises to cut immigration. It was *not* about EU bans on bendy bananas. Unrestricted immigration was a social and political disaster for many people and the government mostly pretended there wasn't a problem. Populism in America was very different but it was obvious that the elites, especially in the Democratic Party, were not listening. *Anybody* could have beaten Donald Trump, *except* Hillary Clinton, but the establishment refused to listen or see. As P.J. O'Rourke aptly noted, 'The American public wasn't holding either political party in much esteem. What the American public was holding was its nose.' To a lesser extent that was true in Britain too.

As the world's most popular current prophet, Yuval Noah Harari, put it in his bestselling *Sapiens,* 'Revolutions are, by definition, unpredictable. A predictable revolution never erupts.' I hesitate to disagree with someone who is considered the wisest sage on earth but I thought Brexit highly possible and could understand why, *before* the vote. I did not think the Americans would vote for Donald Trump, however. By accident almost, Trump, for all his manifest deficiencies, might eventually improve relations with Russia and China. Whether he mends fences, so to speak, with Mexicans or finds jobs for Americans living in the rust belts, is a harder question on which to speculate. And yet despite alarums about North Korea, America is at peace; so is Europe, outside small parts of Ukraine.

To quote from Harari the sage again:

Most people don't appreciate just how peaceful an era we live in. None of us was alive a thousand years ago, so we easily forget how much more violent the world used to be. And as wars become more rare they attract more attention. Many more people think about the wars raging today in Afghanistan and Iraq than about the peace in which most Brazilians and Indians live.

Harari's perspective on violence is an important corrective. It is above all reassuring. Yet his sequel to his bestselling *Sapiens* is *Homo Deus: A Brief History of Tomorrow*. This future vision is not so reassuring, especially when he examines the inevitably massive job losses due to automation. Billions of people will be devoid of any economic or political value. Technological advances may banish death and flesh will become a dead format as humans migrate to cyborg-like creatures with our brains plugged into the Internet. The future, and not so far or sci-fi away, is likely to be consumed with the dangers of controlling artificial intelligence; transcending biology is not yet on our immediate doorstep. Harari is a better historian than he is a scientist, so his first bestseller is far more compelling than his second world-influencing work. One of his points about today is, however, very valid. He said in a recent interview:

> Part of the crisis we are seeing today – like with Brexit, like with Trump in America – is that people are beginning to sense that they are losing power. People make the mistake of blaming 'Brussels' or the 'Washington elite'. This is wrong. Nobody really understands what's happening now in the world, and nobody is in control.

Harari argues that perhaps only Silicon Valley has the faintest idea of what is happening. That may be partly true and an exaggeration because Harari has books to sell. The world has always moved too fast for politicians to keep up. And just as war is too serious to be left to generals, I wouldn't want the future of science to be left in the hands of just clever scientists. The nature of humanity is that there are few easy answers to anything. That of course is the danger of Islam, the fact that the religion disavows all doubt and leaves everything in Allah's hands. It would be comforting to think that Allah, Jehovah or a Church of England feminist gay deity is looking out for us.

Meanwhile we have to do the job ourselves and I think the West is doing OK. I believe Brexit in the longer term will benefit the islands I live in.

Obama's existing legislation and Trump's future laws about those who work and travel in some Muslim countries, as I do, may make it almost impossible for me to visit the USA without more bureaucracy than I want to handle. So I shall now have to look in from outside the universe of the Washington Beltway. I hope Trump improves things. He might be like the sorcerer's apprentice, however, and the sorcerer never returns. Or Trump might be like the Peter Sellers character, Chauncey Gardiner: he might heal Washington, by accident. On the other hand, he could be impeached. His election was as unlikely as the death of some of the drummers in *Spinal Tap*: Trump is so surreal he could even become the victim of spontaneous human combustion. Well, that's what the CIA might announce. And would it be fake news?

Endnotes

Introduction: Saving the West

1. Michael Kranish and Marc Fisher, *Trump Revealed: the definitive biography of the 45th president* (Simon and Schuster, London, 2017) p.364.

Chapter 1: Decline of the West?

1. I am referring specifically to General Sir Richard Shirreff's popular book, *2017: The War with Russia.*

Chapter 2: Law of the Jungle

1. Mark Urban, *The Edge: Is the Military Dominance of the West Coming to an End?* (Little, Brown, London, 2015). This is an excellent short summary of the decline debate.

Chapter 3: 'Always Look on the Bright Side of Life'

1. Yuval Noah Harari, *Sapiens: A Brief History of Humankind,* (Vintage, London, 2011) p.413.
2. Scientists at the University of Warwick used sophisticated technology and complex algorithms to analyse over 8 million books, to measure Britain's happiness since 1776. They discovered that Britain was happiest in 1957, supporting Macmillan's claim. For a summary of the research, see Henry Bodkin, 'Macmillan was right: Britons have never had it so good as in 1957', *Daily Telegraph,* 23 January 2017.
3. Harari, op. cit., p.410.
4. For a good summary of the argument, see David Rothkopf, 'The Case for Optimism: The arc of history bends towards progress – and 2016 was no different'; https://gt.foreignpolicy.com/2016/essay/the-case-for-optimism?df8f7f5682=

Chapter 4: Where did the Islamic State come from?

1. Tom Holland, *In the Shadow of the Sword* (Abacus, London, 2013) p.42.
2. Hugh Kennedy, *The Great Arab Conquests* (Phoenix, London, 2007) p.57.
3. Ibid., p. 376.

4. For example, Jeffrey Lee, *God's Wolf: The Life of the Most Notorious of All Crusaders: Reynald de Chatillon* (Atlantic, London, 2016).

5. Roger Crowley, *City of Fortune: How Venice Won and Lost a Naval Empire* (Faber and Faber, London, 2011) p.315.

6. Officers in the US Marine Corps use a dress weapon which is a scimitar-shaped Mameluke sword because of America's first overseas campaign in Derna, Libya, during the two Barbary wars at the beginning of the nineteenth century.

7. For an excellent summary of Islamic influence on Elizabethan England, see Jerry Brotton, *This Orient Isle: Elizabethan England and the Islamic World* (Allen Lane, London, 2016).

8. For a detailed discussion of British involvement in Egypt and Sudan, see Paul Moorcraft, *Omar al-Bashir and Africa's Longest War* (Pen and Sword, Barnsley, UK, 2015).

9. For more on the what ifs, see Scott Anderson, *Lawrence of Arabia: War, Deceit, Imperial Folly and the Making of the Modern Middle East* (Atlantic, London, 2014).

Chapter 5: Taking on the Islamists

1. See Liam Byrne, *Black Flag Down: Counter-Extremism, Defeating ISIS and Winning the Battle of Ideas* (Biteback, London, 2016).

2. Christopher de Bellaigue, *The Islamic Enlightenment* (Bodley Head, London, 2017).

3. Sara Kahn, *The Battle for British Islam: Reclaiming Muslim Identity from Extremism* (Saqi Books, London, 2016).

4. Allison Pearson, 'Now we must all be brave and confront the ugly truths of Muslim segregation', *Daily Telegraph,* 7 December 2016.

5. Omar Saif Ghobash, *Letters to a Young Muslim* (Picador, London, 2017).

Chapter 6: Dealing with Russia

1. For a modern and accessible discussion of geopolitics, see Tim Marshall, *Prisoners of Geography* (Elliott and Thompson, London, 2016).

2. I was a member of the African section of ARAG.

3. For an interesting study of this subject, see Alistair Horne, *Hubris: The Tragedy of War in the Twentieth Century* (Weidenfeld and Nicholson, London, 2015).

4. General Sir Richard Shirreff, *2017 War with Russia* (Coronet, London, 2016).

Chapter 7: Wider Threats to the West

1. Henry Kissinger, *On China* (Penguin, London, 2012).

2. Niall Ferguson, 'Trump already has his war – it was started in Cyberia and will never end', *Sunday Times* (UK) 12 March 2017.

3. Command, Control, Communications, Computers, Information/Intelligence, Surveillance, Target Acquisition and Reconnaissance.

Chapter 8: Future Options

1. Niall Ferguson, 'At ease, America. Trump's generals are no junta, they are your best hope', *Sunday Times* (UK) 26 February 2017.
2. Bret Stephens, 'Is Europe Helpless?' *New York Times*, 25 July 2016.
3. See, for example, Wolfgang Streeck, *How Will Capitalism End?* (Verso, London, 2016).
4. For a detailed analysis see Brian H. Fishman, *The Master Plan: ISIS, Al-Qaeda, and the Jihadi Strategy for Final Victory* (Yale, London, 2016).
5. Ibid., p.253.
6. Daniel Shillman 'The Muslim World is a Permanent Refugee Crisis', *Frontline Mag*, 25 May 2016.
7. Paul Moorcraft, 'Towards the Garrison State', in F. McA. Clifford-Vaughan, ed, *International Pressures and Political Change in South Africa* (Oxford University Press, Cape Town, 1978).
8. Paul Moorcraft, 'Afghanistan: how to avoid a humiliating defeat by the Taliban', *Business Day,* 1 October 2010.
9. Ralph Peters, 'Blood borders: How a better Middle East would look', *Armed Forces Journal,* 1 June 2006.
10. Robin Wright, 'Imagining a Remapped Middle East', *New York Times, Sunday Review*, 28 September 2013.

Select Bibliography

Ali, Ayaan Hirsi, *Heretic: Why Islam Needs a Reformation Now* (HarperCollins, New York, 2015).

Anderson, Scott, *Lawrence of Arabia: War, Deceit, Imperial Folly and the Making of the Modern Middle East* (Atlantic, London, 2014).

Bellaigue, Christopher de, *The Islamic Enlightenment* (Bodley Head, London, 2017).

Brotton, Jerry, *This Orient Isle: Elizabethan England and the Islamic World* (Allen Lane, London, 2016).

Buchholz, Todd G., *The Price of Prosperity* (HarperCollins, New York, 2016).

Byrne, Liam, *Black Flag Down: Counter-Extremism, Defeating ISIS and Winning the Battle of Ideas* (Biteback, London, 2016).

Chan, Stephen, *Plural International Relations in a Divided World* (Polity, Cambridge, UK, 2017).

Cockburn, Patrick, *The Rise of the Islamic State: ISIS and the New Sunni Revolution* (Verso, London, 2015).

Crowley, Roger, *City of Fortune: How Venice Won and Lost a Naval Empire* (Faber and Faber, London, 2011).

Fishman, Brian H., *The Master Plan: ISIS, Al-Qaeda, and the Jihadi Strategy for Final Victory* (Yale, London, 2016).

Friedman, Tomas L., *Thank you for Being Late* (Allen Lane, London, 2016).

Ghobash, Omar Saif, *Letters to a Young Muslim* (Picador, London, 2017).

Harari, Yuval Noah, *Sapiens: A Brief History of Humankind,* (Vintage, London, 2011).

Hass, Richard, *A World In Disarray: American Foreign Policy and the Crisis of the Old Order* (Penguin, New York, 2017).

Herman, Arthur, *The Idea of Decline in Western History* (Free Press, New York, 1997).

Holland, Tom, *In the Shadow of the Sword* (Abacus, London, 2013).

Houellebecq, Michel, *Submission* (William Heinemann, London, 2015).

Kahn, Sara, *The Battle for British Islam: Reclaiming Muslim Identity from Extremism* (Saqi Books, London, 2016).

Kennedy, Hugh, *The Great Arab Conquests* (Phoenix, London, 2007).

Kissinger, Henry, *On China* (Penguin, London, 2012).

Kranish, Michael and Marc Fisher, *Trump Revealed: the definitive biography of the 45th president* (Simon and Schuster, London, 2017).

Lee, Jeffrey, *God's Wolf: The Life of the Most Notorious of All Crusaders: Reynald de Chatillon* (Atlantic, London, 2016).

Marshall, Tim, *Prisoners of Geography* (Elliott and Thompson, London, 2016).

Moorcraft, Paul, *The Jihadist Threat: The Re-conquest of the West?* (Pen and Sword, Barnsley, UK, 2017).

———, *Dying for the Truth: The Concise History of Frontline War Reporting* (Pen and Sword, Barnsley, UK, 2016).

———, *Omar al-Bashir and Africa's Longest War* (Pen and Sword, Barnsley, UK, 2015).

O'Rourke, P.J., *How the Hell Did this Happen? The US Election of 2016* (Grove Press, London, 2017).

Peters, Ralph, 'Blood borders: How a better Middle East would look', *Armed Forces Journal,* 1 June 2006.

Shillman, Daniel, 'The Muslim World is a Permanent Refugee Crisis', *Frontline Mag*, 25 May 2016.

Shirreff, Richard, *2017 War with Russia* (Coronet, London, 2016).

Streeck, Wolfgang, *How Will Capitalism End?* (Verso, London, 2016).

Urban, Mark, *The Edge: Is the Military Dominance of the West Coming to an End?* (Little, Brown, London, 2015).

Wood, Graeme, 'What Isis Really Wants', *Atlantic Magazine,* March 2015.

Worth, Robert, *A Rage for Order: The Middle East in Turmoil* (Picador, London, 2016).

Wright, Robin, 'Imagining a Remapped Middle East', *New York Times, Sunday Review*, 28 September 2013.

Index